PRIVATE

BY

HAROLD R. PEAT

Ex-Third Battalion First Canadian Contingent

PROFUSELY ILLUSTRATED WITH
PHOTOGRAPHIC REPRODUCTIONS
TAKEN AT THE FRONT.
ALSO WITH SCENES FROM THE PHOTO-PLAY
OF THE SAME NAME
RELEASED BY FAMOUS PLAYERS—LASKY
CORPORATION

1917

British Library Cataloguing-in-Publication Data
A catalogue record for this book is available from the
British Library

Introduction to the

World War One Centenary Series

The First World War was a global war centred in Europe that began on 28 July 1914 and lasted until 11 November 1918. More than nine million combatants were killed, a casualty rate exacerbated by the belligerents' technological and industrial sophistication – and tactical stalemate. It was one of the deadliest conflicts in history, paving the way for major political changes, including revolutions in many of the nations involved. The war drew in all the world's great economic powers, which were assembled in two opposing alliances: the Allies (based on the Triple Entente of the United Kingdom, France and the Russian Empire) and the Central Powers of Germany and Austria-Hungary. These alliances were both reorganised and expanded as more nations entered the war: Italy, Japan and the United States joined the Allies, and the Ottoman Empire and Bulgaria joined the Central Powers. Ultimately, more than 70 million military personnel were mobilised.

The war was triggered by the assassination of Archduke Franz Ferdinand of Austria, heir to the throne of Austria-Hungary, by a Yugoslav nationalist, Gavrilo Princip in Sarajevo, June 28th 1914. This set off a diplomatic crisis when Austria-Hungary delivered an ultimatum to Serbia, and international alliances were invoked. Within weeks, the major powers were at war and the conflict soon spread around the world. By the end of the war, four major imperial powers; the German, Russian, Austro-Hungarian and Ottoman empires—ceased to exist. The map of Europe was redrawn, with several independent nations restored or created. On peace, the League of Nations formed with the aim of preventing any repetition of such an appalling conflict, encouraging cooperation and communication between the newly autonomous nation states. This laudatory pursuit failed spectacularly with the advent of the Second World War however, with new European nationalism and the rise of fascism paving the way for the next global crisis.

This book is part of the World War One Centenary series; creating, collating and reprinting new and old works of poetry, fiction, autobiography and analysis. The series forms a commemorative tribute to mark the passing of one of the world's bloodiest wars, offering new perspectives on this tragic yet fascinating period of human history.

Amelia Carruthers

A Timeline of the Major Events of World War One in Europe

1914

28th June	Franz Ferdinand Assassinated at Sarajevo.
29th June	Austro-Hungary send despatch to Vienna accusing Serbian complicity in the killing.
5th July	Kaiser Wilhelm promises German support for Austria against Serbia.
20th July	Austria-Hungary sends troops to the Serbian frontier.
25th July	Serbia mobilises its troops, Russia sends troops to the Austrian frontier.
28th July	Austria-Hungary Declares war on Serbia.

29th July	Austrians bombard Belgrade and German patrols cross the French border. Britain warns it cannot remain neutral.
1st August	Germany declares war on Russia. Italy and Belgium announce neutrality. French mobilisation ordered.
3rd August	Germany declares war on France and invades Belgium (Schlieffen plan). Great Britain mobilises.
4th August	Britain declares war on Germany and Austria-Hungary (after ultimatum to stand down). US declares neutrality. Germany declares war on Belgium.
6th August	First British casualties with the HMS Amphion sunk by German mines in the North sea. 150 men dead.
7th August	First members of the BEF (British Expeditionary Force) arrive in France.

11th August	Start of enlisting for Kitchener's New Army 'Your King and Country Need You'.
20th August	Brussels is evacuated as German troops occupy the city.
23rd August	The BEF started its retreat from Mons. Germany invades France.
26th August	Russian army defeated at Tannenburg and Masurian Lakes. BEF suffers over 7000 casualties at the Battle of Le Cateau –forced to retreat.
6th September	Battle of the Marne starts; checks German advance, but at the cost of 13,000 British, 250,000 French and 250,000 German casualties.
19th October	First Battle of Ypres.
29th October	Turkey enters the war (on Germany's side).
22nd November	Trenches are now established along the entire Western Front.
8th December	Battle of the Falkland Islands.

1915

19th January	First Zeppelin raid on Britain (Great Yarmouth and Kings Lynn – killing 5).

19th January

First Zeppelin raid on Britain (Great Yarmouth and Kings Lynn – killing 5).

18th February

Blockade of Great Britain by German U-boats begins. All vessels considered viable targets, including neutrals.

22nd April

Second Battle of Ypres begins. Widespread use of poison gas by Germany.

25th April

Allied troops land in Gallipoli.

2nd May

Austro-German offensive on Galicia begins.

7th May

The Lusitania is sunk by a German U-Boat – creating US/German diplomatic crisis.

23rd May

Italy declares war on Germany and Austria

31st May

First Zeppelin raid on London, killing 35 and shaking morale.

30th June	German troops use flamethrowers for the first time, against the British at Hooge, Ypres.
5th August	Germany captures Warsaw from the Russians.
21st August	Final British offensive in the Dardanelles (Scimitar Hill, Gallipoli). They lose, and suffer 5000 deaths.
25th September	Start of the Battle of Loos and Champagne. The British use gas for the first time, but the wind blows it over their own troops, resulting in 2632 casualties.
31st October	Steel helmets introduced on the British Front.
15th December	Sir Douglas Haig replaces Sir John French as Commander of the BEF.

1916

8th January — Allied evacuation of Helles marks the end of the Gallipoli campaign.

21st February — Start of the Battle of Verdun – German offensive against the Mort-Homme Ridge. The battle lasts 10 months and over a million men become casualties. (Finishes 18th December, the longest and costliest battle of the Western Front).

9th March — Germany declares war on Portugal. Six days later, Austria follows suit.

31st May — Battle of Jutland – lasts until 1st June. German High Seas Fleet is forced to retire despite having inflicted heavier losses on the Royal Navy (14 ships and 6,100 men). German fleet irreparably damaged.

4th June — Start of the Russian Brusilov Offensive on the Eastern front. Nearly cripples Austro-Hungary.

1st July	Start of the Battle of the Somme – 750,000 allied soldiers along a 25 mile front. Nearly 60,000 are dead or wounded on the first day.
14th July	Battle of Bazetin Ridge marks the end of the first Somme Offensive. The British break the German line but fail to deploy cavalry fast enough to take advantage. 9,000 men are lost.
23rd July	Battle of Pozières Ridge marks the second Somme Offensive, costs 17,000 allied casualties – the majority of whom are Australian. (ends 7th August).
10th August	End of the Brusilov Offensive.
9th September	The Battle of Ginchy. The British capture Ginchy – a post of vital strategic importance as it commands a view of the whole battlefield.
15th September	First use en masse of tanks at the Somme. The Battle of Flers-Courcelette signifies the start of the third stage of the Somme offensive.

13th November	Battle of Ancre. The fourth phase of the Somme Offensive is marked by the British capturing Beaumont Hamel and St. Pierre Division, taking nearly 4,000 prisoners.
12th December	Germany delivers Peace Note to Allies suggesting compromise.

1917

1st February

Germany's unrestricted submarine warfare campaign starts.

3rd February

US sever diplomatic relations with Germany as U-boats threaten US shipping. Intercepted messages reveal that Germany is provoking the Mexicans into war with the US.

21st February

The great German withdrawal begins. Serre, Miraumont, Petit Miraumont, Pys and Warlencourt are evacuated, falling back 25 miles to establish stronger positions on the Hindenburg Line.

15th March

Tsar Nicholas II abdicates as Moscow falls to Russian Revolutionaries. Demise of the Russian army frees German troops for the Western front.

6th April

USA declares war on Germany – troops mobilise immediately.

9th April	Battle of Arras. British successfully employ new tactics of creeping barrages, the 'graze fuse' and counter battery fire.
16th April	France launches an unsuccessful offensive on the Western Front. – Second Battle of Aisne begins as part of the 'Nivelle Offensive'. Losses are horrendous, triggering mutinies in the French Army.
7th June	The Battle of Messines Ridge. British succeed with few casualties, detonating 19 mines under German front lines – the explosions are reportedly heard from England.
13th June	Germans launch first major heavy bomber raid of London – kills and injures 594.
25th June	First US troops arrive in France.
31st July	Start of the Third Battle at Ypres – a 15 mile front in Flanders. Initial attacks are successful as the German forward trenches are lightly manned.

15th August	The Battle of Lens (Hill 70). – Canadians at the forefront , won a high vantage point, though loss of 9,200 men.
20th August	Third Battle of Verdun begins. French progress is marked by gaining lost territory in the earlier battles.
9th October	The third phase of the Ypres Offensive begins with British and French troops taking Poelcapelle. 25mm of rain falls in 48 hours and the battlefield turns into a quagmire.
12th October	British launch assault at Ypres Against the Passchendale Ridge. New Zealand and Australians take terrible casualties. Bogged down in mud and forced back to start lines.
24th October	Battle of Caporetto – Italian Army heavily defeated.
26th October	Second Battle of Passchendaele begins, 12,000 men lost and 300 yards gained (ends 10th November – 500,000 casualties,

140,000 deaths and 5 miles gained).

6th November | Britain launches major offensive on the Western Front.

20th November | Victory for British tanks at Cambrai - The Royal flying Corps drop bombs at the same time on German anti-tank guns and strong points. Early example of the 'Blitzkrieg' tactics later used by Germany in World War Two.

5th December | Armistice between Germany and Russia signed.

1918

16th January	Riots in Vienna and Budapest with dissatisfaction at the war.
3rd March	Treaty of Brest-Litovsk signed between (Soviet) Russia and Germany.
21st March	Second Battle of the Somme marked by the German spring offensive, the 'Kaiserschlacht'. Germans attack along a 50 mile front south of Arras.
22nd March	Victory for Germany with operation Michael - Use of new 'Storm trooper' assault to smash through British positions west of St. Quentin, taking 16,000 prisoners.
23rd March	Greatest air battle of the war takes place over the Somme, with 70 aircraft involved.
5th April	The German Spring Offensive halts outside Amiens as British and Australian forces hold the Line. The second 1917 battle of

	the Somme ends, as Germany calls off operation Michael.
9th April	Germany starts offensive in Flanders –Battle of the Lys (ends 29th April).
19th May	German air force launches largest raid on London, using 33 aircraft.
27th May	Operation Blucher – The Third German Spring Offensive attacks the French army along the Aisne River. French are forced back to the Marne, but hold the river with help from the Americans.
15th July	Second battle of the Marne started; final phase of German spring offensive. Start of the collapse of the German army with irreplaceable casualties.
8th August	Second Battle of Amiens – German resistance sporadic and thousands surrender.
27th September	British offensive on the Cambrai Front leads to the storming of the Hindenburg Line. Battle of St.

	Quentin – British and U.S troops launch devastating offensives.
4th October	Germany asks the allies for an armistice (sent to Woodrow Wilson).
8th October	Allies advance along a 20 mile front from St. Quentin to Cambrai, driving the Germans back and capturing 10,000 troops.
29th October	Germany's navy mutinies (at Jade).
3rd November	Austria makes peace. German sailors mutiny at Kiel.
9th November	Kaiser Wilhelm abdicates and revolution breaks out in Berlin.
11th November	Germany signs the armistice with the allies – coming into effect at 11.00am (official end of WWI).

1919

10th January	Communist Revolt in Berlin (Battle of Berlin).

10th January — Communist Revolt in Berlin (Battle of Berlin).

18th January — Paris Peace Conference Begins.

25th January — Principle of a League of Nations ratified.

6th May — Under conditions of the Peace conference, German colonies are annexed.

21st June — The surrendered German naval fleet at Scapa Flow was scuttled.

28th June — Treaty of Versailles signed.

19th July — Cenotaph unveiled in London.

By Amelia Carruthers

Memoirs, Diaries and Poems of World War One

In 1939, the writer Robert Graves was asked to write an article for the BBC's *Listener* magazine, explaining 'as a war poet of the last war, why so little poetry has so far been produced by this one.' From the very first weeks of fighting, the First World War inspired enormous amounts of poetry, factual analysis, autobiography and fiction - from all countries involved in the conflict. 2,225 English war poets have been counted, of whom 1808 were civilians. The 'total' nature of this war perhaps goes someway to explaining its enormous impact on the popular imagination. Even today, commemorations and the effects of a 'lost generation' are still being witnessed. It was a war fought for traditional, nationalistic values of the nineteenth century, propagated using twentieth century technological and industrial methods of killing. Memoirs, diaries and poems provide extraordinary insight into how the common soldier experienced everyday life in the trenches, and how the civilian population dealt with this loss.

Over two thousand published poets wrote about the war, yet only a small fraction are still known today. Many that were popular with contemporary readers are now obscure. The selection, which emerged as orthodox during the 1960s, tends to (understandably) emphasise the horror of war, suffering, tragedy and anger against those that wage war. This was not entirely the case however, as demonstrated in the early weeks of the war. British poets responded with an outpouring of patriotic literary production. Robert Bridges, Poet Laureate, contributed a poem *Wake Up England!* calling for 'Thou careless, awake! Thou peacemaker, fight! Stand, England, for honour, And God guard the Right!' He later wished the work to be suppressed though. Rudyard Kipling's *For All We Have and Are,* aroused the most comment however, with its references to the 'Hun at the gate... the crazed and driven foe.'

From Hemingway's *A Farewell to Arms,* to Remarque's *All Quiet on the Western Front,* to the poetry of Sassoon, Graves, and Brooke, there are numerous examples of acclaimed writing inspired by the Great War. One of the best known war poets is perhaps Wilfred Owen, killed in battle at the age of twenty-five. His poems written at the front achieved popular attention soon after the war's end, most famously including *Dulce Et Decorum Est, Anthem for Doomed Youth,* and *Strange Meeting.* In preparing for the publication of his collected poems, Owen explained 'This book is not about heroes. English poetry is not yet fit to speak of them. Nor is it about deeds, or lands, nor anything about glory, honour, might, majesty, dominion, or power, except War. Above all I am not concerned with Poetry. My subject is War, and the pity of War. The Poetry is in the pity.'

Dulce et Decorum Est, one of Owen's most famous poems, scathingly takes Horace's statement, 'Dulce et decorum est, pro patria mori', meaning 'It is sweet and proper to die for one's country' as its title. It chiefly describes the death of an anonymous soldier due to poison gas, vividly describing the suffering of the man, ending with a bitter attack on those who see glory in the death of others. Such themes were also widely utilised by authors unaccustomed with the literary canon - the common soldier noting down their experiences for their loved ones, and for posterity. Each unit in World War One was in fact required to keep a diary of its day-to-day activities, many portraying the anxiety and terror of the opening days of the war. Diaries from soldiers in the First Battalion South Wales Borderers (among others, recently released at the British National Archives) described the battles of the Marne and the Aisne, with one captain who said the scenes he witnesses were 'beyond description... poor fellows shot dead are lying in all directions... everywhere the same hard, grim pitiless sign of battle and war. I have had a belly full of it.'

Other, lighter aspects of everyday life including tugs of war, rugby matches and farewell dinners to mark the end of the fighting have also been documented, giving us a rare insight into what the First World War was like for the men on the front line. Letters were an incredibly important part of life as a soldier. Receiving and writing them helped keep them sane, and could take them away from the realities of trench life. Every week, an average of 12.5 million letters were sent to soldiers by family, friends, and partners. More formalised memoirs have also become a key way of understanding the conflict, from gas attacks, the fear of going over the top, methods of coping with death - as well as the jovial camaraderie which often grew up between the men. The first memoirs of combatants were published in 1922, not long after the armistice: *A Tank Driver's Experiences* by Arthur Jenkins and *Disenchantment* by Charles Edward Montague. These were shortly joined with *Good-Bye to All That* (1929) by Robert Graves, *A Subaltern's War* (1929) by Charles Edmund Carrington, and *Blasting and Bombardiering* (1937) byPercy Wyndham Lewis. Nurses also published memoirs of their wartime experiences, such as *A Diary without Dates* (1918) by Enid Bagnold, and *Forbidden Zone* (1929) by Mary Borden. Vera Brittain's *Testament of Youth* (first published 1933) has been acclaimed as a classic for its description of the impact of the war on the lives of women and the civilian population - extending into the post-war years.

Storm of Steel, written by Ernst Jünger, published in 1920 was one of the first personal accounts to be published - a graphic account of trench warfare, unusually glorifying the sacrifice encountered. The book has consequently been criticised for lionizing war, especially when compared with works such as Remarque's (albeit fictional) *All Quiet on the Western Front.* In the preface to the 1929 English edition, Jünger stated that; 'Time only strengthens my conviction that it was a good and strenuous life, and that the war, for all its destructiveness, was an incomparable schooling of the heart.' As is evident from this short introduction to the memoirs, diaries, letters and poems of the first world war

- it is an intensely complex field. Dependent on military rank, geographic position and placement, nationality and subjective experience and character, they take on a wide variety of forms and focuses. Such works give an amazing insight into the experiences of combatants and it is hoped the current reader is encouraged to find out more about this thoroughly worthwhile topic.

Amelia Carruthers

Image 1. Canadian troops leaving for France

The Western Front

The First World War was one of the deadliest conflicts in history. More than seven million civilians and nine million combatants were killed, a casualty rate exacerbated by the belligerents' technological and industrial sophistication – and tactical stalemate. It lasted four years, however nobody expected the war to be more than a short, decisive battle. Following the outbreak of war in 1914, the German Army opened the Western Front by first invading Luxembourg and Belgium, then gaining military control of important industrial regions in France. Battle raged until the end of the war in 1918 when the German government sued for peace, unable to sustain the massive losses suffered. The western front included some of the bloodiest conflicts of the war, with few significant advances made; among the most costly of these offensives were the Battle of Verdun with a combined 700,000 dead, the Battle of the Somme with more than a million casualties, and the Battle of Passchendaele with roughly 600,000 casualties.

The massive tide of initial German advance was only turned with the Battle of the Marne, when the German army came within 70km of Paris. This, first battle of the Marne (5th-12th September 1914) enabled French and British troops to force the German retreat by exploiting a gap which appeared between the first and second Armies. The German army retreated north of the Aisne River and dug in there, establishing the beginnings of a static western front that was to last for the next three years.

Following this German setback, the opposing forces tried to outflank each other in the Race for the Sea, and quickly extended their trench systems from the North Sea to the Swiss frontier. As a result of this frenzied race, both sides dug in along a meandering line of fortified trenches, stretching all the way along the front - a line which remained essentially unchanged for most of the war.

Between 1915 and 1917 there were several major offensives along this front. The attacks employed massive artillery bombardments and massed infantry advances. However, a combination of entrenchments, machine gun nests, barbed wire, and artillery repeatedly inflicted severe casualties on the attackers and counterattacking defenders. In an effort to break the deadlock, the western front saw the introduction of new military technology, including poison gas, aircraft and tanks. Although all sides had signed treaties (the Hague Conventions of 1899 and 1907) which prohibited the use of chemical weapons in warfare, they were used on a large scale during the conflict. This was most evident at the Second Battle of Ypres (21 April – 25 May 1915), an offensive led by the Germans in order to disrupt Franco-British planning and test a relatively new weapon; chlorine gas. The Germans released 168 tons of this gas onto the battlefield, creating panic amongst the British soldiers - many of whom fled creating an undefended 6km wide gap in the Allied line.

The Germans were unprepared for the level of their success however and lacked sufficient reserves to exploit the opening. Canadian troops quickly arrived and drove back the German advance. It was only after the adoption of substantially revised tactics that some degree of mobility was restored to the front. The German Spring Offensive of put such ideas to good use, with recently introduced infiltration tactics, involving small, lightly equipped infantry forces attacking enemy rear areas while bypassing enemy front line strong-points and isolating them for attack by follow-up troops with heavier weapons. They advanced nearly 97km to the west, which marked the deepest advance by either side since 1914 and very nearly succeeded in forcing a breakthrough. The German Chief of Staff, Erich von Falkenhayn, believed that a breakthrough might no longer be possible, and instead focused on forcing a French capitulation by inflicting massive casualties. The new goal was to 'bleed France white.'

This policy resulted in the Battle of Verdun, which began on 21st February after a nine-day delay due to snow and blizzards. To inflict the maximum possible casualties, Falkenhayn planned to attack a position from which the French could not retreat for reason of both strategic positions and national pride - Verdun was an important stronghold, surrounded by a ring of forts, guarding the direct route to Paris. The French put up heavy resistance though, and halted the German advance by 28th February. Over the summer they slowly advanced with the use of the rolling barrages and pushed the Germans back 2km from their original position. This battle, known as the 'Mincing Machine of Verdun' became a symbol of French determination and self-sacrifice. The futility and mass slaughter of the war was perhaps nowhere better illustrated than in the Battle of the Somme however; convened to help relieve the French after their enormous losses at Verdun.

Here, British divisions in Picardy launched an attack around the river Somme, supported by five French divisions on their right flank. The attack was preceded by seven days of heavy artillery bombardment, which failed to destroy any of the German defences. This resulted in the greatest number of casualties (killed, wounded, and missing) in a single day in the history of the British army, about 57,000. By August 1916, General Haig, like Falkenhayn, concluded that a breakthrough was unlikely, and instead switched tactics to a series of small unit actions (similar to the German infiltration tactics). The final phase of the Somme also saw the first use of the tank on the battlefield, which did make early progress (4km), but they were mechanically unreliable and ultimately failed. All told, the battle which lasted five months only succeeded in advancing eight kilometres, at a truly massive loss to life. The British had suffered about 420,000 casualties and the French around 200,000. It is estimated that the Germans lost 465,000, although this figure is controversial.

This constant loss of life meant that troop morale became incredibly low. The Nivelle Offensive, primarily including French and Russian troops - which promised to end the war within forty-eight hours, was significant failure. It took place on rough, upward sloping terrain, tiring the men - whose troubles were increased due to poor intelligence and German control of the skies. Within a week, 100,000 French troops were dead and on 3rd May, an entire division refused their orders to march, arriving drunk and without their weapons. Mutinies then spread and afflicted a further fifty-four French divisions, only stopped by mass arrests and trials. Such low morale was further dampened by the German's final spring offensives which very nearly succeeded in driving the allies apart

Operation Michael (March 1918), the first of these German offensives advanced 100 km, getting within shelling distance of Paris for the first time since 1914. The allies responded with vigour however, with a counter-offensive at the Marne, followed by an attack at Amiens to the North. This attack included Franco-British forces, and was spearheaded by Australian and Canadian troops, along with 600 tanks and supported by 800 aircraft. The assault proved highly successful, leading Hindenburg to name 8 August as the 'Black Day of the German Army.' These losses persuaded the German government to sue for armistice, and the Hundred Days Offensive (beginning in August 1918) proved the final straw. Many German troops surrendered, although fighting did continue until the armistice was signed on 11th November 1918. The war in the Western Front's trenches left a generation of maimed soldiers and grieved populations, though proved a decisive theatre in ending the First World War. The repercussions of this bloody conflict are still being felt to this day. It is hoped the current reader is encouraged to find out more, and enjoys this book.

Amelia Carruthers

In Flanders Fields

In Flanders fields the poppies blow
Between the crosses, row on row,
That mark our place; and in the sky
The larks, still bravely singing, fly
Scarce heard amid the guns below.

We are the Dead. Short days ago
We lived, felt dawn, saw sunset glow,
Loved and were loved, and now we lie
In Flanders fields.

Take up our quarrel with the foe:
To you from failing hands we throw
The torch; be yours to hold it high.
If ye break faith with us who die
We shall not sleep, though poppies grow
In Flanders fields.

John McCrae, May 1915

"There were many words that you could not stand to hear and finally only the names of places had dignity. Abstract words such as glory, honor, courage, or hallow were obscene."

American novelist and WW1 veteran Ernest Hemingway, in 'A Farewell to Arms', 1929

PRIVATE PEAT

To the boys who will never come back

Private Peat Still smiling though his right arm is useless

FOREWORD

In this record of my experiences as a private in the great war I have tried to put the emphasis on the things that seemed to me important. It is true I set out to write a book of smiles, but the seriousness of it all came back to me and crept into my pages. Yet I hope, along with the grimness and the humor, I have been able to say some words of cheer and comfort to those in the United States who are sending their husbands, their sons and brothers into this mighty conflict. The book, unsatisfactory as it is to me now that it is finished, at least holds my honest and long considered opinions. It was not written until I could view my experiences objectively, until I was sure in my own mind that the judgments I had formed were sane and sound. I give it to the public now, hoping that something new will be found in it, despite the many personal narratives that have gone before, and confident that out of that public the many friends I have made while lecturing over the country will look on it with a lenient and a kindly eye.

To my wife, who has helped me greatly and who has been my inspiration in this, as in all else, I should have inscribed this volume had she not urged the present dedication. But she prefers it as it is, for "the boys who will never come back" gave themselves for her and for all sister-women the world over.

H.R.P.

PRIVATE PEAT

CHAPTER I

THE CALL—TO ARMS

"Well," said old Bill, "I know what war is ... I've been through it with the Boers, and here's one chicken they'll not catch to go through this one."

Ken Mitchell stirred his cup of tea thoughtfully. "If I was old enough, boys," said he, "I'd go. Look at young Gordon McLellan; he's only seventeen and he's enlisted."

That got me. It was then that I made up my mind I was going whether it lasted three months, as they said it would, or five years, as I thought it would, knowing a little bit of the geography and history of the country we were up against.

We were all sitting round the supper table at Mrs. Harrison's in Syndicate Avenue, Edmonton, Alberta. War had been declared ten days before, and there had been a call for twelve hundred men from our city. Six hundred were already with the colors.

Now, to throw up a nice prosperous business and take a chance at something you're not sure of getting into after all, is some risk, and quite an undertaking as well. But I had lived at the McLellens' for years and knew young Gordon and his affairs so well that I thought if he could tackle it, there was no reason why I shouldn't.

"Well, Bill, I'm game to go, if you will," I said. Bill had just declared his intention rather positively, so I was a bit surprised when he replied in his old familiar drawl:

"All right, but you'll have to pass the doctor first. I'm pretty sure I can get by, but I'm not so certain about you."

Ken Mitchell looked up at that and, smiling at me, said, "I can imagine almost anything in this world, but I can't imagine Peat a soldier."

"Well, we'll see about that, Ken," I replied, and with that the supper came to an end.

That evening Bill and I went over to the One-Hundred-and-First Barracks, but there was nothing doing, as word had just come from Ottawa to stop recruiting. It was on the twenty-second of August, 1914, before the office was opened again, and on that day we took another shot at our luck.

The doctor gave me the "once over" while Bill stood outside.

"One inch too small around the chest," was the verdict.

"Oh, Doc, have a heart!"

"No," he said, "we have too many men now to be taking a little midget like you." That was disappointment number two. I walked out and reported to Bill, and I need not say that that loyal friend did not try to pass without me.

That night—August twenty-second—I slept very little. I had made up my mind that I was going to the war, and go I would, chest or no chest. Before morning I had evolved many plans and adopted one. I counted on my appearance to put me through. I am short and slight. I'm dark and curly-haired. I can pass for a Frenchman, an American, a Belgian; or at a pinch a Jew.

I had my story and my plan ready when the next day I set out to have another try. At twelve-thirty I was seated on Major Farquarhson's veranda where I would meet him and see him alone when he came home to lunch.

"Excuse me, Doctor," I said when he appeared, "but I'm sure you would pass me if you only knew my circumstances."

"Well?" snapped the major.

"You see, sir, my two brothers have been killed by the Germans in Belgium, and my mother and sisters are over there. I *must* go over to avenge them."

I shivered; I quaked in my shoes. Would the major speak to me in French? I did not then know as much as *Bon jour.*

But luck was with me. To my great relief Major Farquarhson replied, as he walked into the house, "Report to me this afternoon; I will pass you."

August 28, 1914, saw old Bill—Bill Ravenscroft—and me enlisted for the trouble.

A few days later Bill voiced the opinion of the majority of the soldiers when he said, "Oh, this bloomin' war will be over in three months." Not alone was this Bill's opinion, or that of the men only, but the opinion of the people of Canada, the opinion of the people of the whole British Empire.

And right here there lies a wrong that should be righted. From the days of our childhood, in school and out, we are taught what WE can do, and not what the other fellow can do. This belief in our own strength and this ignorance of our neighbor's follows us through manhood, aye, and to the grave.

It was this over-confidence which brought only thirty-three thousand Canadian men to the mobilization camp at Valcartier, in answer to the first call to arms, instead of the one hundred thousand there should have been.

Not many days passed before we boarded the train at Edmonton for our journey to Valcartier. The first feeling of pride came over me, and I am sure over all the boys on that eventful Thursday night, August 27, 1914, when thousands of people, friends and neighbors, lined the roadside as we marched to the station.

Only one or two of us wore the khaki uniform; the rest were in their oldest and poorest duds. A haphazard, motley, rummy crowd, we might have been classed for anything but soldiers. At least, we gathered this from remarks we overheard as we marched silently along to the waiting troop-train.

Strangely enough no one was crying. Every one was cheered. Little did hundreds of those women, those mothers, dream that this was the last look they would have at their loved ones. Men were cheering; women were waving. Weeping was yet to come.

On that same August night, not only from Edmonton, but from every city and town in Canada men were marching on their way to Valcartier.

We traveled fast, and without event of importance. There were enthusiastic receptions at each town that we passed through. There was Melville and there was Rivers, and there was Waterous, where the townsfolk declared the day a public holiday, and Chapelou in Northern Ontario, where we had our first parade of the trip. There was a tremendous crowd to meet us here, a great concourse of people to welcome these stalwarts of the West. We lined up in as good formation as possible, and our sergeant, who was very proud of himself and of us— mostly himself—majestically called us to attention.

"From the left, number!" he gave the command. Such a feat, of course, is an impossibility.

"From the right, Sergeant," yelled old Bill.

"No," answered the sergeant, "from the left." The crowd roared and the sergeant raved. Finally our captain straightened us out, but the sergeant to this day has never forgotten the incident.

North Bay passed, then Ottawa, Montreal, and at last we arrived at Valcartier. So far the life of a soldier had been anything but a pleasant one. My body was black and blue from lying on the hard boards, and I was eager, as was every other man, to leave the train at once; but as our camp was not quite ready we had to stay in the cars another night.

It was a relief, I assure you, when on the morning of September first we marched into Valcartier. Such a sight: tents everywhere one looked; all around little white marquees. I said to Bill, "Is this the regular training ground?" To my surprise he informed me that this great camp had been organized within the last two weeks.

I marveled at this for I did not believe we had a man in Canada with the organizing ability to get a camp of this size in such splendid shape in so short a time. We were finally settled in our quarters and told that we were to be known as the Ninth Battalion, One-Hundred-and-First Edmonton Fusiliers.

The second day we were in camp the bugle sounded the assembly. Of course I did not know an "assembly" from a mess call, but the others ran for the parade ground and so I followed.

Gee! what a mob! There was a big man sitting on a horse. Bill said he was the colonel. He made a speech to us. He told us we were fine men.

"You are a fine body of men," said he ... "but we are unorganized, and we have no non-commissioned officers."

I whispered to Bill, "What's a non-commissioned officer?"

Bill looked to see if I really meant it. "A sergeant, a corporal—anything but a private," he replied.

"Will all the men who have had former military experience fall out," commanded the colonel; "the rest of you go back to quarters."

"Have I had any former military experience, Bill?" I was eager for anything.

"Sure you have," said Bill. "We'll just stay here and maybe we'll be made sergeants."

About six hundred of us stayed! But, believe me, if they had all had as much military experience as I, we wouldn't have been soldiers yet. When the adjutant came around, he gave me a look as much as to say: "That kid certainly has got a lot of nerve." He offered to make Bill a corporal, but as that would have transferred him from D Company to F Company he declined rather than leave me.

This will give you some idea of the kind of organization or non-organization when the First Contingent Canadians was formed. Not only in our own battalion but nearly anywhere in the regiment almost anybody could have been a non-commissioned officer—certainly anybody that had looks and the nerve to tell the adjutant that he had had former military experience.

It was not very long before we began to realize that soldiering, after all, was no snap. There was the deuce of a lot to learn, and the deuce of a lot to do.

To the rookie one of the most interesting things are the bugle calls. The first call, naturally, that the new soldier learns is "the cook-house," and possibly the second is the mail-call. The call that annoyed me most at first was "reveille." I had been used to getting up at nine o'clock in the morning; rising now at five-thirty wasn't any picnic. This, especially when it took a fellow half the night to get warm, because all we had under us was Mother Earth, one blanket and a waterproof.

It was the second day at camp that we started in to work good and hard. Reveille at five-thirty a.m.; from six to seven Swedish exercise, then one hour for breakfast when we got tea, pork and beans, and a slice of bread. From eight to twelve saw us forming fours and on the right form companies. From twelve to half past one more pork and beans, bread and tea. Rifle practise, at the butts, followed until five-thirty, and ... yes, it did ... pork and beans, bread and tea appeared once more.

Neither officers nor non-coms knew very much at the start, but they were a bunch of good scouts. And we were all very enthusiastic, there is no doubt about that. Soon we began to realize that if we would put our shoulders to the wheel and work hard we would certainly see service overseas.

©Famous Players—Lasky Corporation. Scene from the Photo-Play THE SONS OF DEMOCRACY.

Honorable discharge service button given to Canadians who have seen actual service in France.

MRS. HAROLD R. PEAT

Badges from tunics of dead comrades.

Identification disk now worn around the neck.

Souvenirs brought back from "Over There." The enemy calls the Canadian a "Souvenir Hunter." It must be remembered the author is a Canadian.

As a private soldier and no matter how humble my opinion may be, I must give the greatest praise and credit to the organizer and founder of Camp Valcartier, at that time Colonel Sir Sam Hughes ... the then minister of militia for Canada. We had about three miles of continuous rifle range; and good ranges they were, considering they were got together in less than two weeks. I will admit that the roads leading to the ranges were nothing to brag about, yet, taking it all in all, even they were pretty good.

By this time the majority of us had received our uniforms and our badges, and had been given a number, and instructed to mark this number on everything we had. Mine was 18535.

We had no "wet" canteens at Valcartier, so we were a very sober camp. Each battalion had a shower bath, and there was no excuse for any man to be dirty. Even at that it was not very long before those little "somethings" which are no respecters of persons, be he private, non-com, commissioned officer or general, found their way into the camp. I'll never forget the first gray-back I found on me. I cried like a baby, and old Bill sympathized with me, saying in consoling tones that I'd soon get used to them. Bill knew.

For amusement at Valcartier, we had free shows and pay shows, also moving pictures. The pay show got to be so amusing that we made a bonfire out of it one bright September night, and found it more entertaining as a conflagration than it ever had been as an entertainment. At all events, that was how one of the boys of the Fifteenth Battalion put it.

The second week in camp we were inoculated, and again examined for overseas service. Through some very fine work, I escaped the examination, but could not get out of the inoculation. We were promised three shots in the arm, but after the first I resolved that one was more than enough for me. German bullets could not be worse, I thought, and when I got one I didn't change my mind.

As the days wore on we grew more and more enthusiastic. Already rumors were spreading that we would be leaving "any time now" for France. The excitement certainly told on some of the boys. In my regiment no less than nine, I guess they were ex-homesteaders, went "nutty." One chap, I recall, killed hundreds of Germans on the bloody battle-fields of Valcartier. The surgeon assured us the mania was temporary.

We were pretty thoroughly equipped by the end of the third week, when we were given puttees instead of leggings. It was sure funny the way some of the boys looked when they first put them on, for many of them got the lower part of the leg much bigger than the upper part, but of course that might happen to any one who had never seen puttees before.

There was considerable grumbling about these same puttees, because, at first, they were undoubtedly very uncomfortable. However, before many days the majority of us were ready to vote for puttees permanently, as they proved warmer, a greater support to the leg on long marches and more nearly waterproof than their more aristocratic brother leggings.

It was during the third week of camp life that we had our first review. We gave the salute to the Duke of Connaught, who was accompanied by Sir Sam Hughes. After this review, we were told that we might expect to leave for France at two hours' notice.

The following days we spent on the rifle ranges and in making fake departures. I wrote home to my friends more than once that "we were leaving for the front to-day," but when the next day arrived we were still leaving. I sent my mother six telegrams on six different days to say that I would start for France within the next hour, but at the end of it we were still to be found in the same old camp.

Finally, on the first day of October, 1914, our regiment boarded the *S.S. Zeeland* at Quebec. The comment of the people looking on was that they had never seen a finer body of men. And that was about right. Physically we were perfect; morally, we were as good as the next, and, taken all in all, there were no better shots on earth. Equipped to the minute, keen as hunting dogs, we were "it." Surely a wonderful change this month's training had wrought. And I say again if the credit for it all must be given to any one man, that man is Sir Sam Hughes.

In a few hours we were steaming down the St. Lawrence, and the next day we slipped into Gaspé Bay on the eastern coast of Canada, where we joined the other transports. Here thirty-two ships with as many thousand men aboard them were gathered together, all impatiently waiting the order to dash across the Atlantic.

We did not have to wait very long. On Sunday, October the fourth, at three o'clock in the afternoon, we steamed slowly out of the harbor in three long lines. Each ship was about a quarter of a mile from her companion ahead or behind, and guarded on each side by cruisers. I have memorized the names of the transports, and at this time it is interesting to know that very few of them have been sunk by the German submarines.

The protecting cruisers were: *H.M.S. Eclipse, Diana, Charybdis, Glory, Talbot* and *Lancaster*. The transports were in Line Number One: *S.S. Manatic, Ruthenian, Bermudian, Alaunia, Irvenia, Scandinavian, Sicilia, Montzuma, Lapland, Casandia;*

Line Number Two: *Carribean, Athenia, Royal Edward, Franconia, Canada, Monmouth, Manitou, Tyrolia, Tunissian, Laurentic, Milwaukee;* Line Number Three: *The Scotian, Arcadian, Zeeland, Corinthian, Virginian, Andania, Saxonia, Grampian, Laconia, Montreal, The Royal George.*

All the way across the Atlantic we were in sight of each other and of the cruisers. Personally, the scene thrilled me through and through. Here was the demonstrated fact that we, an unmilitary people, with a small population to draw on, had made a world record in sending the greatest armada that had ever sailed from one port to another in the history of man. Personally, I felt very proud because of the thirty-three thousand soldiers on these boats only seventeen per cent. were born Canadians; five per cent. Americans, and the other seventy-eight were made up of English, Irish and Scotch residing in Canada at the outbreak of the war.

There were no exciting scenes on the way over, except when some wild and woolly Canadian tried to jump overboard because of seasickness. We were a long time crossing, because the fastest transport had to cut her speed down to that of the slowest, and the voyage was anything but a pleasant one. When we finally steamed into Plymouth, the gray-backs outnumbered the soldiers by many thousands. The invasion of England!

CHAPTER II

IN THE OLD COUNTRY

We were the first of the British Colonial soldiers to come to the aid of the Motherland. Judging from the wonderful reception given us, it was easy to see that the people were very pleased at our coming, to put it mildly.

My first night on English soil I shall never forget. After three weeks on ship coming over, we were all pretty stiff. The night we landed in England we marched many miles, and as a result my feet were awfully sore. So, when we finally arrived at Salisbury Plain and were immediately ordered to march across the Plain another ten miles to Pond Farm, I knew I shouldn't be able to do it, and confided my troubles to Bill and another fellow named Laughlin. After we had gone about four miles we came to an inviting haystack; it was too much for us and all three of us slipped out of line, but before we could reach the stack we were caught by Major Anderson. Bully old major! He volunteered to carry my pack. In turn, I carried his greatcoat, and we continued the march.

It wasn't very long before another haystack came in view and again we couldn't resist the temptation. This time we made our goal, and there we slept until early morning. Thus I passed my first night on English soil. Two days later we landed in camp, after visiting Devizes, Lavington and Salisbury City on the way. Laughlin wore the major's coat, and by this device got through where otherwise we should have been pinched.

After the first two days in England it began to rain, and it kept on raining all the time we were there. The people round about the country told us that never before in their lives had they seen such rains, but this must be characteristic of people the world over. In Western Canada when strangers come and it gets really cold, we tell the same story of never having seen the like before.

We hadn't been in camp long when they began to issue passes to us. The native-born Englishmen were the first to get leave, and the Canadians next. At last my turn came, but unfortunately I had to go alone. Personally, I think the English people made too big a fuss over us. The receptions we got at every turn of the way were stupendous; and I am certain a majority of the men had more money than was really good for them. As one young Canadian boy said afterward: "Why, they treated us as if we were little tin gods."

But from a military view-point, we, the boys of the First Canadian Division, did not make such a tremendous hit with British officials. It was not long before they even criticized us openly, and looking at it from a distance I do not blame them. Never in their lives had they seen soldiers like us. They had been used to the fine, well-disciplined, good-looking English Tommy. Of course I will admit that we were good-looking all right, but as far as discipline was concerned, we did not even know it by name. The military authorities could not understand how it was that a major or a captain and a private could go on leave together, eat together and in general chum around together.

The English people, I dare say, had read a lot about the wild and woolly West, but now in many instances they had it brought right home to Piccadilly and the Strand. With a band of young Canadians on pass, I assisted once in giving Nelson's Monument in Trafalgar Square the "once over" with a monocle in my left eye. A few hours later this same crowd commandeered a dago's hurdy-gurdy, and it was sure funny to see three Canadian Highlanders turning this hand organ in Piccadilly Circus.

The folks, of course, took all these little pranks good-naturedly; and, as a Canadian, I can not speak too highly of the treatment handed out to us by the Britishers. If there ever was a possibility before this war of Canada's breaking away from the Motherland, such a possibility has been shot to the winds. No two peoples could be more closely allied than we of the West and they of this tiny but magnificent island.

The little training we had had in Canada was good, as far as it went, and we had devoured it all. But the most vital part of a soldier's up-bringing was absolutely forgotten by our officers—discipline! As I've said before, as far as discipline was concerned, we were a joke. Certainly we were looked upon as such by the Imperial officers.

In one of the leading British weeklies there appeared a series of comments reflecting rather seriously on our discipline. One of the most humorous yet caustic, it seemed to me, was of an English soldier on guard at a post just outside of London. His instructions were to stop all who approached. In the darkness it was impossible for him to distinguish one person from another. Before long he heard footsteps coming toward him:

"Halt! Who goes there?" demanded the sentry.

"The Irish Fusiliers," was the answer.

"Pass, Irish Fusiliers; all's well."

Before long some more steps sounded....

"Halt! Who goes there?"

"The London Regiment."

"Pass, Londons; all's well."

"Halt! Who goes there?"

"Hic ... mind your own damn business...."

"Pass, Canadians; all's well."

At a parade, one bright November morning, when we were at Salisbury, a certain brigadier-general from Ontario, since killed in action, while reviewing the soldiers of a particular battalion, made a unique speech to the boys when he said:

"Lads, the king and Lord Kitchener and all the big-bugs are coming down to review us to-day, and for once in your lives, men, I want to see you act like real soldiers. When they get here, for the love o' Mike, don't call me Bill ... and, for God's sake, don't chew tobacco in the ranks."

There is no doubt about it, the authorities probably looked on us as a bunch of good fellows, but that's about all.

While still in England, all the men of the First Canadian Contingent were issued a cloth lapelette or small shoulder strap; the infantry, blue; the cavalry, yellow with two narrow blue stripes; the artillery, scarlet, and the medical corps, maroon. I was told that these lapelettes were given to distinguish us from other contingents. To-day there are only a few hundred men entitled to wear what now amounts to a badge distinction. Personally, I feel prouder of my blue lapelette than of anything else I possess in the world.

The so-called training that we were supposed to have in England was not really any training at all. The rain was almost continuous, we were constantly being moved from one camp to another, and training, as training is understood to-day, was out of the question.

As I have said, our first camp in England was Pond Farm. It was well named. Later we moved to Sling Plantation. However, it was at Pond Farm we had some of our most grueling experiences. Many a night, owing to the awful rains, we would have to move our tents sometimes in the middle of the night. If any minister of the gospel—except our chaplain—had been standing around on these occasions he might well have thought from the sulphurous perfume of the air that every soldier was doomed to everlasting Hades. But, after all, "cussing" is only a small part of a soldier's life, and who would not swear under such extraordinary circumstances? Again, we have authority for it. It is a soldier's commandment on active service—the third commandment—and here is how it reads:

"Thou shalt not swear unless under extraordinary circumstances."

An "extraordinary circumstance" can be defined as moving your tent in the middle of the night under a downpour of rain, seeing your comrade shot, or getting coal oil in your tea. As a matter of fact, all minor discomforts in the army are counted as "extraordinary circumstances."

Despite the weather conditions, and the fact that we did very little training, the men in our battalion were enthusiastic and did their best to keep fit. However, we all went to pieces when we were told, early in December, that it was a cinch our battalion would never get to France as a unit.

I'll never forget the day our captain broke the news to us. The tears ran down his cheeks, and he wasn't the only man who cried. We were almost broken-hearted to know we were to be divided, because Captain Parkes (now Colonel) was a real and genuine fellow. He had taught us all to love him. For instance, when after a long march we would come in with our feet blistered, he would not detail a sergeant to look after us. He would, himself, kneel down on the muddy floor and bathe our feet. If at any time we were "strapped" and wanted a one-pound note, we always knew where to go for it. It was always Captain Parkes, and he never asked for an I.O.U. either. On the gloomy wet nights of the winter he would play games with us, and it was common to hear the boys remark that if we should ever get to France as a unit, and our captain got out in front, it would not be one man who would rescue him, but the whole company.

The day at Pond's Farm was more than a sad one when the old Ninth was made into a Reserve Battalion. The men were so greatly discouraged and the sergeants so grouchy that at times it became almost humorous.

One day, in late December, while at the butts, we were shooting at six hundred yards, with Sergeant Jones in command of the platoon. We had targets from Number One to Number Twenty inclusive, and the men were numbered accordingly. At this distance we all did fairly well, except Number One, who missed completely. For the sake of Number One the sergeant moved us down to four hundred yards, and at this distance every man got a bull's eye except Number One. He was off the target altogether. Our sergeant, after a few very pungent remarks, commanded the section to move to one hundred yards. Here again each one of us had a bull to his credit but Number One. Again he had missed, and again we moved, this time to fifty yards.

At fifty yards I can not begin to describe the look on the sergeant's face—to say that his eyes, nose and mouth were twitching is putting it mildly. Nevertheless, Number One missed. Then, something that never happened before on a rifle range on this earth electrified us all. Sergeant Jones shouted at the top of his voice: "Number One, attention! Fix bayonet! Charge! That's the only d——d hope you've got."

Disappointments were frequent enough in camp. Take the case of the Fifth Western Cavalry, who could sport the honor of their full title on their shoulder straps in bold yellow letters. It was they who had to leave horses behind and travel to France to fight in what they termed "mere" infantry. To this day we know them as the "Disappointed Fifth." There was also the Strathcona

Horse of Winnipeg who were doomed to disappointment and much foot-slogging with their horses left behind.

Among those made into reserve units we of the Ninth had for companions the Sixth, Eleventh, Twelfth and Seventeenth Battalions. It was obvious that somebody had to be kept in reserve, and we were the unlucky dogs. We cursed our fate, but that didn't mend matters. We had nothing for it but to trust to a better fortune which should draft us into a battalion going soon to the fighting front.

The First Brigade consisted of men of the First, Second, Third and Fourth Battalions of Infantry. All of these battalions came from Ontario. The Second Brigade was made up of men from the West, including Winnipeg, Regina, Saskatoon, Calgary and Vancouver. They were in the Fifth, Seventh, Eighth and Tenth Battalions, all infantry.

The Third Brigade was commonly known as the Highland Brigade and was made up of the Thirteenth, Fourteenth, Fifteenth and Sixteenth Battalions. This last brigade included such splendid old regiments as the Forty-Eighth Highlanders of Toronto, the Ninety-First Highlanders of Hamilton and Vancouver, and the Black

Watch of Montreal. There were also some of the far eastern men in this brigade.

After all this rearrangement had been made, it was only a few days till the rumor flew about that the battalions might leave for France at any time now. It seemed to us poor devils of the old Ninth that everything was going wrong. The unit lying next to us, the Seventeenth Battalion, was quarantined with that terrible disease, cerebro-spinal-meningitis. For a few days we buried our lads by the dozen. Speaking for myself, my nerves were absolutely unstrung, and I am sure that most of the men were in the same condition. It can be easily understood then that when drafts were asked for, to bring up the regiments leaving for France to full strength, there was a mad scramble to get away.

Without even passing the surgeon, I finally drifted into the Third Battalion, ordinarily known as the "Dirty Third." This battalion was made up of the Queen's Own, the Bodyguards and Grenadier Regiments of Toronto.

I landed in on a Sunday afternoon about three o'clock and was immediately told by the quartermaster that we were leaving for France in a few hours. He told me that I needed a complete change of equipment. At this news I rejoiced, because so far we had all worn, in our battalion, the leather harness known as the "Oliver torture." I knew that the active service, or web, equipment could not be worse.

The rush for equipment issue was like a mêlée on the front line after a charge, as I found out later on. There were some three hundred men newly drafted into the Third Battalion; there were some three hours in which we had to get our equipment and learn to adjust it. As it was, many of the extreme greenhorn type marched away garbed in most sketchy fashion. Some had parts of their equipment in bags; others utilized their pockets as holders for unexplained, and to them inexplicable, parts of the fighting kit.

Another of our trials was the new army boot. In Canada we had been issued a light-weight, tan-colored shoe, more practicable for dress purposes than for active service. Now we had the heavy English ammunition boot. This is of strong—the strongest—black leather. The soles are half-inch, and they are reenforced by an array of hobnails. These again are supplemented by tickety-tacks, steel or iron headed nails with the head half-moon shape. Each heel is outlined with an iron "horse shoe." Until the leather has been softened and molded with much rubbing and the unending use of dubbing, I would say, mildly, that these boots are not of the easiest.

Our departure for France was thrilling in its contrasts. Before setting out we cleaned camp, and then we had a fine speech from our new commander, Colonel Rennie, of Toronto, of whom much was to be heard in the hard days to come.

We slipped out of the camp in silence and utter darkness. Troops were being moved through England and into France with the utmost secrecy. We dare not sing as we marched; we dare not speak to a neighbor. On and on, it seemed endless, through mud and water and mud again. At times it reached to our knees as we plowed our way to the railway, where trains with drawn blinds awaited us.

Before we were half through our march a terrific electrical storm broke over us; the thunder roared and the lightning split the sky open as though Heaven itself were making a protest against war.

We finally embarked on *His Majesty's Transport Glasgow*.

CHAPTER III

BACK TO CANADA—I DON'T THINK

It was seven in the evening before we were ready to start. At that hour we quietly slipped our anchor and glided out of the harbor. We all thought we would be in France before midnight. The trip across the Channel in ordinary times is not often more than two and a half hours. We had no bunks allotted to us, and didn't think that any would be needed. We all lay around in any old place, and in any old attitude. I, for one, devoted most of the time during that evening to learning the art of putting my equipment together. The majority of the boys were at the old familiar game, poker.

We had not been on this transport very long when we had our first introduction to bully beef and biscuits. Bully beef is known to civilians the world over as corned beef, and to the new Sammy as "red horse." But even bully beef and biscuits aren't so bad, and our thoughts were not so much on what we were getting to eat as on when we were getting to France.

As the hours went by we more and more eagerly craned our necks over the deck rails, trying to pierce the darkness of the deep for one flash of light that might mean France hard ahead. But nothing happened, and one after another the watchers dropped off to sleep.

When dawn broke we woke and rubbed our eyes. We were mystified and not a little mortified. Where was France? There was nothing but water, blue as heaven itself, around us. We were still at sea, and still going strong.

The hours of that day dragged out to an interminable length. No one spoke of the matter—the question of land in sight was not discussed. Some of the boys went back to poker. Others decided to be seasick, and subsequently wished for a storm and the consequent wrecking of the ship, with a watery death as relief.

Bully beef and biscuits at noon; bully beef and biscuits at our evening meal, and no sight of land. Night came. The more hopeful of us did the craning business over the deck rails for a few more hours. The pessimistic, deciding France had ceased to be, returned to poker. We slept. We woke. We watched the sun rise—over the sea!

About noon that day after the ration of bully beef had gone its round and we, in consequence, were feeling pretty blue, there was a group of us standing around doing nothing. Suddenly Tom King came rushing up in great excitement. He had had an idea.

"Say, you fellows, I don't care a darn what any of you may say, I believe these blinkin' English are sick of us and are sending us back to Canada!"

No such luck. Before sundown that evening we sighted land. We steamed slowly into the port of St. — —. This is a large seaport town near the Bay of Biscay, on the southwest coast of France. Why in the world they wanted to take us all the way round there, I don't know. I was told that we were among the first British troops to be landed at this port.

As soon as we disembarked from the boats that evening, before we left the docks, we were issued goat-skin coats. The odor which issued from them made us believe that they, at least in some former incarnation, had belonged to another little animal family known as the skunk. Ugh! The novelty of these coats occupied us for a while, and if a sergeant or a comrade addressed us we answered in "goat talk": "Ba-a-a, ba-a-a-a...."

It was apparent that the secrecy of troop transportation which held in England held also in France. The populace could not have known of our coming, for there no scene, nor was there a reception. We were to meet with that later on.

Here, however, we did meet the French "fag." When Tommy gets one puff of this article of combustion he never wants another. It is one puff too many. Of course our first race was to buy cigarettes—but, napoo!

Before entraining we were all shocked by the dreadful tidings that the transport carrying the Forty-Eighth Highlanders had been sunk. This news was soon discredited and the truth was established when the Forty-Eighth came up the line in a few days and reported that they had heard *we*, the Third, had been sunk and all drowned. Apparently it was a part of certain propaganda to publish that all transports of British soldiers were destroyed. So far none had even been attacked.

The evening of our arrival we boarded the little trains. To our surprise and to our intense disgust, we had not even the passenger coaches provided in England and Canada. I say little trains, because they were little, and in addition the coaches were not coaches, but box cars. Painted on the side of the "wheeled box" was "*Huit chevaux par ordinaire.*"

But these are not ordinary times, so instead of eight horses they put forty-eight of us boys in each car. Forty-eight boys all my size might have worked out well enough, though in full fighting trim even I was quite a husky, but the average Canadian soldier is a much bigger man. Take into consideration what we have to carry. There is our entrenching tool which we use for digging in. To look at it the uninitiated might well think that it was a toy, but, as I learned afterward, when bullets are flying around you by the thousand you can get into the ground with even a toy—or less.

There is our pack. A soldier's pack on active service in the British Army is supposed to weigh approximately forty-five pounds, but when the average Tommy lands in France his pack weighs nearer seventy-five pounds than forty-five. Tommy does not feel like throwing away that extra pair of boots, two or three suits of extra underwear, and so many of the little things sent from home or given him just before setting out for France. As a consequence when he arrives in France he carries a very heavy load, though it does not stay heavy for long. After being on a route march or two the weight will mysteriously disappear. Then Tommy carries one pair of boots, one suit of underwear, one shirt, one pair of socks, and they are all on him.

There is a mess tin to cook in, wash in, shave in and do all manner of things with. There is the haversack in which is stuffed a three-day emergency ration. The emergency ration of the early days of the war was much different from the emergency ration of to-day. These rations are intended to be used only in an emergency, and, believe me, only in an emergency are they used. There was compressed beef—compressed air, we called it; there were Oxo cubes and there was tea. In addition there were a few hardtacks.

Then there is the bandoleer, and the soldier on active service in this war never carries less than one hundred and fifty rounds of ammunition at any one time, and sometimes he carries much more. As a final, there is our rifle and bayonet. At that time of which I am speaking we Canadians carried the now famous, or infamous, Ross rifle. This weighed nine and three-quarters pounds.

With all this equipment to a man, and forty-eight men to each small box car, it doesn't demand much imagination to picture our journey. We could not sit down. If we attempted it we sat on some one, and then there was a howl. We tried all manner of positions, all sorts of schemes. In the daytime we sought the roof of the cars, or leaned far out the open doors. If the country had not been so lovely, and if all our experiences had not been new and out of the ordinary, there would have been more grousing.

The second day on the train—we were three days and three nights—while passing through a city near Rouen, we had a glimpse of our first wounded French soldiers. It seemed as though war came home to a lot of us then for the first time. I was fairly sick at heart when I saw one Frenchman with both arms bound up, and with blood pouring over his face. I understood that these wounded men were coming back from the battle of Soissons. From the glimpses we caught of them in their train they seemed a funny lot of fighting men, these poilous, with their red breeches, their long blue coat pinned back from the front, the little blue peaked cap, and their long black whiskers. I was horrified at the whole sight. For the first time I asked myself, "What in the world are *you* out here for?"

There must have been many of the boys who indulged in the same vein of thought, to judge by the seriousness of the faces as we proceeded and left the French hospital train behind.

On the evening of the third day, as we pulled slowly into the station at Strazeele, we could hear in the distance the steady rumbling of the big guns at the front.

CHAPTER IV

ARE WE DOWNHEARTED? NO!

"Hush, boys,... we're in enemy country!" our second in command whispered ominously. We shivered. The sound of the guns seemed to grow louder. Captain Johnson repeated his warning:

"Not a word, men," he muttered, and we stumbled out of the station in silence that could be cut with a knife. Sure enough the enemy was near. He couldn't have been less than twenty-two miles away! We could hear him. There was no disposition on our part to talk aloud. Captain Johnson said: "Whisper," and whisper we did.

We trekked over mud-holes and ditches, across fields and down through valleys. We had many impressions— and the main impression was mud. The main impression of all active service is—mud. It was silent mud, too, but we knew it was there. Once in a while during that dark treading through an unfamiliar country one of the boys would stumble and fall face down. Then the mud spoke ... and it did not whisper. There were grunts and murmurings, there were gurgling expletives and splutterings which sent the army, and all fools who joined it, to places of unmentionable climatic conditions. We were in it up to our necks, more or less literally.

All the way along we could see the flashes of star shells. When one went up we could fancy the battalion making a "duck" in perfect unison. The star shells seemed very close. It was still for us to learn that they always seem close.

After about seven miles of this trekking, we reached billets. This was our first experience of French billets. The rest-house was a barn and we were pretty lucky. We had straw to lie on.

Notwithstanding our distance from the enemy, as Captain Johnson had said, we were in his country, and in consequence there had to be a guard. Four of the boys were picked for the job. There was no change in my luck. I was one of the chosen four.

The guardroom, whether for good or ill, was set in a chicken house. And thereby hangs a tale—feather. Corporal of the guard was a sport. He was a young chap from Red Deer, Alberta. Now, figure the situation for yourself. For days past we had been feeding on bully beef—bully beef out of a tin. Four men on guard, a dozen chickens perched not a dozen feet away. Would abstemiousness be human? Ask yourselves, *mes amies.*

We drew lots. My luck had turned. But I ate of it. It was tender; it was good; it was roasted to a turn.

They say dead men tell no tales. Of dead chicken there is no such proverb. Wish there had been. We buried those feathers deep. Alas, that Monsieur, in common with all the folk in Northern France, was so thorough in his cataloguing of his properties. I don't blame him. He had dealt with Germans when they overran the territory. He had met with Belgians when they hastened forward. He had had experience of his own countrymen when they endeavored to drive back the enemy. He had billeted the Imperial British soldier. Now he was confronted with a soldier of whom he had no report, save only the name—Canadian. Monsieur had counted his chickens before they were perched.

We had not yet had read or explained to us the laws and penalties attaching to such a crime while on active service. Of course, no one killed that chicken. No one ate it. No one knew anything about it. We were perfectly willing, if need be, to pay double price for the chicken rather than have such a term as "chicken thief" leveled at us. We of the guard, however, protested, but paid five francs each to smooth the matter over. This totaled about four dollars.

The next morning the whole battalion was lined up before the colonel while the adjutant read aloud the law which we boys term the "riot act." This document informed us very clearly that if any soldier was found to have taken anything from the peasantry for his own use; if any man was found drunk on active service, or if he committed any other crime or offense which might be counted as minor to these two, the punishment for a first offense would be six months first field punishment. For any offense of a similar nature thereafter the man would be liable to court martial and death.

While this paper was being read, I shook in my boots, to think that I had been—innocently or at least ignorantly—associated with what was probably the first crime of our battalion.

On our way

We went back to billets a very subdued lot of soldiers.

Later in the day I noticed a lot of boys talking to a young Belgian girl. I had no opportunity to speak to her then, but after a time I found her alone, and with the little English Mademoiselle Marie B—— had picked up from British soldiers lately billeted there, and with the small amount of French I had stored away, we held quite a long conversation.

©Famous Players—Lasky Corporation. Scene from the Photo-Play THE VOICE OF THE TEMPTER.

I should judge that she was about fifteen. She told me she was sixteen. She was piquant and pretty in appearance, but her features were drawn and her expression was sad. She had a questioning wistfulness in her eyes, but she showed no fear of the many British soldiers round.

This young girl, little over a child, was all alone. She awaited in terror the coming of her baby, and the fiends who had outraged her had brutally cut off her right arm just a little above the elbow.

"How did this happen to you, Mademoiselle?" I asked in French.

"Ah, Monsieur," she replied, "*les Allemands*, they did—chop it off."

"Why, Mademoiselle, surely no German would do such a hideous thing as that without some reason."

At that time I believed, as apparently do the majority of people in this country to-day believe, that the Germans did not commit the atrocities that were attributed to them. But it is all true.

"But, *oui*, Monsieur,... *les Allemands*, they have no reason. They kill my two brothers ... my father I have not seen, my mother I have not seen ... no, not for five months. *Les Allemands*, they have taken them also ... they are dead also, *peutetre*."

"And you?" I continued. "Where was your home?"

"Ah, but it is the long story. We live close by Liége. It is a small village. The Uhlans come and we are sorely frightened. We hide in the cellar, and do not go out at all. While there *les Allemands* post a notice in the village. It is that every person who has a gun, a pistol, a shell, an explosive, must hand such over to the burgomaster. We do not know of this, and do nothing. At last, Monsieur, the Uhlans come to our house to search, and there they see a shotgun and some shot. It is such a gun as you must know in the house of British, in the house of American. It is the common gun. We did not know. But there is no pardon for ignorance in war. My brothers were roughly pulled to the market place and shot dead." Little Marie choked down a sob. "My mother and my father," she continued, "were carried away. I refuse. I fight, I bite, I scratch, I scream with frenzy, I tear. One of *les Allemands* ... perhaps he was mad, Monsieur, he slash ... so, and so ... he cut off my arm.

"I remember no more, Monsieur. After a day ... two days, I find that I can walk. I walk and walk. It is now one hundred and fifty miles from my home ... it is that I stay here until...."

I grasped the girl's left hand and turned away. I was sick. What if she had been my sister?

And then I thought of the laws read aloud to us that morning. We soldiers, fighting under the flag of the British Empire, were we to violate one little rule ... were we to take any property, no matter how small, without just payment to its owner; were we to drink one glass of beer too much ... were we to overstep by a hair's breadth the smallest rule of the code of a "soldier and a gentleman," we were liable to be shot.

What of the German who had ruined this young girl and maimed her body? Believe me, I realized then, if never before, what we were fighting for. I was ready to give every drop of blood in my veins to avenge the great crimes that this little girl, in her frail person, typified.

We passed another night in the same billets. Next morning at five-thirty we were roused to make a forced march, across country, of some twenty-two miles. This was the hardest march of the entire time I was at the front. Those ammunition boots! Those gol-darned, double distilled, dash, dash, dash, dashed boots!

It was winter. There was heavy traffic over the roads. There were no road builders, and precious little organization for the traffic. Part of the way the surface had been cobblestones; now it was broken flints.

We started out gallantly enough with full packs, very full packs. Then, a few miles out, one would see out of the corner of his eye, a shirt sail quietly across the hedge-row; an extra pair of boots in the other direction; another shirt, a bundle of writing paper; more shirts, more boots. Packs were lightening. Down to fifty pounds now; forty, thirty, twenty, ten ... the road was getting worse.

No one would give up. Half a dozen men stooped and slashed at their boots to get room for a pet corn or a burning bunion. But every man pegged ahead. This was the first forced march. We were on our way to the trenches. No man dare run the risk of being dubbed a piker. We agonized, but persevered.

Armentières was our objective. A fine city, this, and one which we might have enjoyed under happier circumstances. It was under fire, but not badly damaged, and consequently many thousands of the Imperial soldiers were "resting" there while back from the trenches.

We were the First Canadians. We were expected, and the English Tommies determined to give us right royal welcome and a hearty handshake. We had a reputation to keep up, for in England the Cockney Tommy and his brother "civvies" had named us the "Singing Canydians."

But on the road to Armentières ... oh, *ma foi!* There was no singing. Call us rather the "Swearing Canydians," as we stumbled, bent double, lifting swollen feet, like Agag, treading on eggs through the streets of the city.

Tommy Atkins to right of us; Tommy Atkins to left of us, cobblestones beneath us, we staggered and swayed. The English boys cheered and yelled a greeting. It was rousing, it was thrilling, it was a welcome that did our hearts good; but we could not rise to the occasion.

Suddenly from out of the crowd of khaki figures there came a voice—that of a true son of the East End—a suburb of Whitechapel was surely his cappy home.

"S'y, 'ere comes the Singin' Can-ydians ... 'Ere they come ... 'Ear their singin'."

Not a sound from our ranks. Silence. But it was too much. No one can offer a gibe to a man of the West without his getting it back. Far from down our column some one yelled:

"Are we downhearted?" "No!" We peeled back the answer raucously enough, and then on with the song:

Are we downhearted? No, no, no.
Are we downhearted? No, no, no.
Troubles may come and troubles may go,
But we keep smiling where'er we go,
Are we downhearted? Are we downhearted?
No, no, *NO!*

"No, Gor'blimey, y'er not down'earted, but yer look bally well broken-'earted," chanted our small Cockney comrade, with sarcasm ringing strong in every clipped tone of his voice.

CHAPTER V

UNDER FIRE

Broken-hearted! Gee! We sure were—nearly; but not quite. No. This was bad; there was worse to come, and still we kept our hearts whole.

But there was another trial now, and we were directed to rest billets in what presumably had been a two-story schoolhouse or seminary. As soon as we reached this shelter we flopped down on the hard bare floor and lay just as we were, not even loosening our harness.

We were less than three miles from the front lines. Even at this short distance Armentières, as a whole, had not suffered greatly from shell fire, though the upper floors of this old seminary had been shattered almost to ruins long before our arrival.

The city itself was a good strategic point for the artillery. Behind houses, stores, churches, anywhere that offered concealment, our guns were hidden. Our artillery officers used every available inch of cover, for they had to screen our guns from the observation of enemy aircraft which flew with irritating irregularity over the town, and they had to avoid the none too praiseworthy attention of spies, in which Armentières was rich.

Armentières in those days was practically a network of our gun emplacements. The majority were howitzers. These fire high; they have a possible angle of forty-five degrees. There was no danger of their damaging our own immediate positions.

The ordinary infantry man knows less than nothing about artillery. If ever a bunch of greenhorns landed in France, frankly, we of the First Contingent were that same bunch.

As we had marched through the city there had been no sound of gun-fire. All was quiet except for the welcoming cheers of our British brothers. Silence reigned for the two hours we had spent in resting on the floor of the schoolhouse, and consequently we thought we had a snap as far as position went.

Our self-congratulations were somewhat rudely disturbed. Of a sudden, one of our young officers rushed through the door of our shelter. Poor laddie, he was very young and his anxiety exceeded even his nervousness. Nervousness is very natural, I can assure you. It is natural in a private; it is more so in the officer who feels responsibility for the lives of his men.

"Lads," said he, with upraised hand, and obviously trying desperately to be calm, "lads, I've just been told that the enemy has the range of this building. 'Twas shelled yesterday, and we are likely to be blown up any minute ... any minute, men! I'd advise you to stay where you are. Don't any of you go outside, and if you don't want to lose your lives, don't go fooling around upstairs." With that he pointed to the rickety steps that led to the second floor and disappeared through the door as fast as he had come.

For a few moments there was dead silence. "Blow up any minute!" We looked at one another. We sat tense. Our very thoughts seemed petrified. From the far corner of the room there came a sound:

"Gee whiz!... Gee whiz!" the voice gathered confidence. "Gee whiz, guys"—it was a boy from the Far West who spoke—"I've come six thousand miles, and to be blown up without even seeing a German is more than I can swallow."

"Gosh!" said I, "I wouldn't mind being shot tomorrow morning at sunrise if I could have the satisfaction of seeing one of them first."

Bob Marchington looked up. He was a droll youth, and curiosity was his besetting sin. "Say, fellows, I wonder why he told us not to go up-stairs. I bet you there's something to be seen from up there, or he would not have told us not to go. Any of you boys willing to come up with me?"

No one took up the challenge. We lay around a little longer. Then the braver spirits commenced to deliberate on the suggestion. Why not go up-stairs? At last half a dozen of us decided to embark on the risky enterprise. We were three miles from the enemy, to be sure, but a German at three miles seemed to us then something formidable. Many a good laugh have we had since, in trench and out, at this expedition considered with so much careful thought!

We crept up the shaky steps one by one. We crawled along the upper floor, skirting the gaping shell holes in the woodwork. We raised our hands and shaded our eyes from the glare of the light. We scanned the horizon. We had an idea, I think, that we'd see a German blocking the landscape somewhere. We were three miles away. What was three miles to us?

We were deeply engrossed when there came a terrific crash. It seemed almost under our feet ... Rp-p-p-p-p-p bang, BANG! The next thing I remembered was landing at the foot of those narrow stairs, the other five boys on top of me. That is a feat impossible of repetition. When we disentangled ourselves, got to our feet and gathered our scattered wits, we found the men who had remained below tremendously excited. Their hair was on end; their eyes were like saucers. "Who's killed, fellows," they yelled, "who's killed?"

Of course no one was hurt. Our own battery was just dropping a few over the Boches, but it was our first experience under fire. Behind the building a battery of our six-inch howitzers was concealed. When they "go off" they make a fearful racket; very likely any other bunch of fellows, not knowing the guns were there, would do as we did. I don't know. At all events, we stayed very quietly where we were thereafter.

Later in the evening we found out the true and inner meaning of the excited order not to go outdoors or on the roof. It was a simple device to keep us from exploring the boulevards of the city. We might have been tempted to do that, for we had seen none of the charming French girls as yet, and they are—*tres charmante.*

About six o'clock that evening we got the customary—the eternal—bully beef and biscuits. At seven we were ordered to advance to the front line trenches. Our captain gathered us around him. He wanted to talk to us before we went "in" for the first time. He was, possibly, a little uncertain of our attitude. He knew we were fighters all right, but our discipline was an unknown quantity. Captain Straight, I understand, was American-born, from Detroit, Michigan. We liked him. Later we almost worshiped him. We took all he said to heart. We listened intently; not a word did we miss. I can repeat from memory that pre-trench speech of his.

"Boys," the captain's voice was solemnity itself. "Boys, to-night we are going into the front line trenches. We are going in with soldiers of the regular Imperial Army. We are going in with seasoned troops. We are going in alongside men who have fought out here for weeks. We've got to be very careful, boys."

Our captain was obviously excited. We strained closer to him.

"You don't know a darn thing about war, lads ... I know you don't."

We fell back a pace somewhat abashed. We had been under fire that very afternoon; but the captain (fortunately) did not know it.

"You don't know the first thing about this war. You've not had opportunities of asking about it from wounded men. Now, boys, I know exactly what you are going to do to-night when you get in those trenches. You're going to ask questions of those English chaps. YOU ARE NOT." He emphasized every one of those three words with a blow of one fist on the other.

"You are not. Why, men, you know what the authorities think of our discipline. How are we to know that this is not a device to try our mettle. How are we to know that those boys already in are not there to watch us, to report our behavior ... and, by heaven, men, if we don't make a good showing perhaps they will report unfavorably on us; perhaps we will be shipped out of here, shipped back to Canada, and become the laughing stock of the world."

Captain Straight strode up and down. "It won't do, my lads. You must not ask questions. Why, men, let those English fellows ask *you* the questions. Don't you speak at all ... just you be brave. I know you *are* brave ... stick out your chests." The captain gave us an illustration. We all drew ourselves up; we almost burst the buttons from our tunics in our endeavor to expand ... with bravery.

"Keep your heads high," the captain went on, one word tripping the other in the eagerness of his speech. "March right in. Don't stop for anything. Get close to the parapet. Look at the British boys; throw them 'Hello, guys!' and begin to shoot right away."

We were ready for anything. Were we not brave? Hadn't we shown our bravery by creeping up a ruined stairway only three miles from the enemy? We promised our captain, and then we commenced our march to the front.

The green soldier is always put into the first line at the start. The general idea is that he should be put in reserves and worked up gradually, but, save under exceptional circumstances, he is put in the front line and worked back.

It has been demonstrated that shell fire is much more severe on a man's nerves than rifle fire. Reserve trenches suffer more from shell fire than do the front line trenches. The reason is obvious. Sometimes the front line is but a stone's throw from the front line of the enemy. Sometimes we can converse with the enemy from one trench to the other. In such cases it is impossible for heavy artillery to be trained on the front. Rifles and bombs are the only explosives under these conditions.

Again, the green soldier is never put into the trenches alone. A company of raw arrivals is sandwiched in with seasoned men. As we were the first Canadians to arrive, and there was none of our own men to help acclimatize us, we went in with an English regiment. There was one English, one Canadian and so on down the line. These boys belonged to the Notts and Derbys. Jolly fine boys, too. We became fast friends. They chummed to us as they would to their own. They showed us the ropes. They gave us tips on this thing and that. They told us the best way to cook, the various devices for snatching a few minutes' rest. They described the most effective "scratching" methods for the elimination of "gray-backs," "red-stripes," "cooties," "crawlies"—any name you like to give those hosts of insect enemies that infest every trench.

Now, "going in" isn't so easy as it sounds. We don't advance in companies four deep. We don't have bands. We don't have pipes to inspire our courage and rouse the fighting spirit inherited from long dead ancestors. It is a very—a vastly different matter. We go into the trenches in single file, each man about six paces from his nearest comrade. There is no question about keeping behind. Instinct takes care of that.

A man may have a touch of lumbago; he may have a rheumatic pain. None of these things matters to him on the way "in." He can bend his back quickly enough as he passes along. There are always a few bullets dropping near by. One will hit the mud somewhere around his feet. The boy nearest springs as from a catapult until he is close to the comrade ahead of him. No; he never springs back. If he did ... he would be the man ahead. He would be in front. Nuffin' doin'—the whole idea is to keep behind; there is no doubt of that.

But the guide is very vigilant. All troops are guided to their positions, and the man on this ticklish job is nearly always a sergeant. He has an eagle eye, and a feline sense of hearing. He will note your skip forward.

"Keep your paces, lads ... keep your paces." His voice booms altogether too loud for us.

"Hush! for the love o' Mike, Sergeant, not so loud." He chuckles. He knows that feeling so well, so awfully well now. He has been a guide these many times. But we skip back to our position, six paces behind. Then another bullet drops and the whole dance-step is repeated with little variation. The sergeant booms once more, and in desperation that the Boches will hear him, we obey.

'Tis pretty how we step, too, on that first time "in." We lift each foot like a trotting thoroughbred. We step high, we step lightly. We tread as daintily as does a gray tomcat when he encounters a glass topped wall on a windy night.

CHAPTER VI

THE MAD MAJOR

This first night in, had the commander-in-chief, had any one who questioned the discipline of the First Canadians, seen us, he would have been proud of our bearing, our behavior.

The Tommy who has been there before, when on guard never shows above the parapet more than his head to the level of his eyes. When he has had his view on the ground ahead, he ducks. He looks and ducks frequently. But we—we were not real soldiers; we were super-soldiers. We were not brave; we were super-brave. We went into those trenches; we returned the greeting of the English boys; we lined up to the parapet; we stretched across it to the waistline, and then rose on tippy-toe. I do admit it was a very dark night; at least it appeared so to me. Oh, we were on the brave act, all right, all right.

We stood there staring steadily into the blackness. Suddenly a bullet would come "Zing-g-g-g," hit a tin can behind us, and then we would duck, exclaim "Good lord! that was a close one," then resume the old position. But we soon· learned not to have many inches of our bodies displayed, target-fashion, for the benefit of the Dutchies.

The first night in we fired more bullets than on any other night we were at the front. We saw more Germans that night. They sprang up by dozens; they grew into hundreds as the minutes passed and the darkness deepened. We felt like the prophet Ezekiel as he viewed the valley of dry bones. There was the shaking, there was the noise, and my imagination, at least, supplied the miraculous warriors. It was an awful night, that first night in.

Any one knows that if frightened in the dark (we were not frightened, of course; only a little nervous), the worst thing to do is to keep the eyes on one spot. Then one begins to see things. It is not necessary to be a soldier, and it is not necessary to go to the front line in France to make sure of that statement. Stare ahead into the dark anywhere and something will move.

We had our eyes set, and we peppered away. An English officer strolled by, and addressed a fellow near me. "What the ... what the blinkety-blank are you shooting at?"

"Me, sir ... m-me, sir? Germans, sir...." And he went on pumping bullets from his old Ross. The officer smiled.

For myself, I was detailed for guard. I stood there on the firestep with my body half exposed. I did not feel very comfortable. I thought if I could get any other job to do, I would like it better. The longer I stayed, the more certain I became that I would be killed that night. I did not want to be killed. I thought it would be a dreadful thing to be killed the first night in. A few bullets had come fairly close—within a yard or two of my head. I determined there and then, should opportunity offer, I would not stay on guard a minute longer than I could help.

My chance came sooner than I had hoped for. I hadn't realized, what I discovered after a few more turns in the trenches, that guard duty is the easiest job there is. I was eager for a change, and when I heard an English sergeant call out: "I want a Canadian to go on listening-post duty," I hopped down from my little perch and volunteered: "I'll go, Sergeant. Take me."

I had my job transferred in a few minutes. I honestly did not know the duty for which I was wanted. I knew there was a ration back in the town. I had a vague idea that we would go back to the town for more bread or something of the kind.

I had heard of an outpost, but a listening-post was a new one on me. These were very early days in the war. The Imperial soldiers had recently established this new system, and as yet it was not a matter of common knowledge.

This war is either so old-fashioned in its methods or so new-fashioned—in my opinion it is both—that it is continuously changing. The soldier may be drilled well in his own land, if he comes from overseas; he may be additionally trained in England; he may have a couple of weeks at the base in France, but it is all the same—when he reaches the front line trenches there will have been a change, an improvement, in some thing or other. It may be but a detail, it may be but a new name for an old familiar job, but changed it is.

The best soldier in the fighting to-day is the type of man who can adapt himself to anything. He must have initiative; he must have resource; he must have individuality; he must be a distinct and complete unit in himself, ready for any emergency and any new undertaking.

I started promptly to hike down the communication trench, following back the way we had come. An English private soldier was detailed to go on listening-post with me. Again, the raw soldier is never left to his own devices on first coming in. He is given the support of a veteran on all occasions, unless under some very special condition.

"Hie!" called the private to me, "where're yer goin' to?"

"Back, ye bally ass!"

He looked his contempt. "'Ave yer b'ynet fixed?" he asked, by way of answer.

"Bayonet fixed?"

"Yes," said he, "'urry up! We're late."

"Late?" I repeated.

"For Gawd's syke," he exclaimed, "don't yer know as 'ow we are goin' hout? Goin' over to the German trenches—goin' hout!"

©Famous Players—Lasky Corporation. Scene from the Photo-Play THE END OF A PERFECT DAY.

Cheerful beggars

I gulped. "Going to make a charge?"

"No ... goin' HOUT ... listenin'-post." And that private started out across No Man's Land as nonchalantly as though he were strolling along his native strand. I followed. I followed cautiously. I don't know how I got out. I don't remember. I can't say that I was frightened ... no, I was just scared stiff. Five paces out I put my hand on the Englishman's shoulder ... I was quite close to him; don't doubt it. He stopped.

"How far is it to the German trenches?" I whispered.

"Eh?"

I raised my voice just a trifle. I didn't know who might hear me: "How far is it to the German trenches?"

"Five 'undred yards." My companion started off again. He stepped on a stick. I jumped. I jumped high. We continued, then I stopped him once more.

"Are we alone out here? Are there any Germans likely to be out too?"

"Why, yes ... plenty of 'em out here."

"Do they go in pairs, like us; or have they squads of them...."

"Pairs, my son, pairs, brace, couples...." The private strode on.

"Do our boys ever meet any of the Boches?"

"Sure! Many a time."

"What do we do?"

"Do? Stick 'em, matey, stick 'em! You've learnt to use yer b'ynet, 'aven't yer? Well, stick 'em ... kill 'em! Don't use yer rifle ... the flash would give you away, and then ye'd be a corpse."

I felt I was a corpse already. I felt that if there was any killing to be done that night he would have to do it, not I.

We crept more cautiously now. My comrade did not tread on sticks. I whispered to him for the last time: "What are we out here for, anyway?"

Then he explained. He was a good-hearted chap. "Don't yer know w'ot listenin'-post is? W'y, there's a couple of us fellows hout at intervals all along the line. We get as close to the enemy parapet as is possible. We watch and listen, lyin' flat on the ousey ground hall the while. We are the heyes of the harmy. The Germans raid us on occasions. Were these posts not hout, the raids would be more frequent. They'd come hover and inflict severe casualties on hour men. They can't see the Boche. We can. Should one Boche, or five 'undred try to come hover that parapet, one of us must immediately set hout and run back to hour trenches and give the warnin' for hour boys to be ready. The other one of us stays back 'ere, and with cold steel keeps back the rush."

I nodded. "What happens afterward to the man who stays back here?"

"Mentioned in despatches ... sometimes," Tommy returned casually.

I thought over the matter. Tommy whispered further.

"Oh, yer needn't be a bit nervous. There's two of us lads about every forty or fifty yards. This is the w'y. 'Ere we are, 'ere the Boches are ... there the boys are"—he flicked an expressive thumb backward. "Those Boches thinks as 'ow they 'as to get to our trenches, but before they gets to our trenches, they 'as to pass us ... they 'as to pass US ... see?"

I saw. "Say," I touched him gently, "a while before I joined up, I did the hundred yards in eleven seconds flat ... those Boches may pass you to-night, but never, on your life, will they pass me."

Tommy chuckled. He had been through it all himself. Every man has it the first time that he goes on any of these dangerous duties. I can frankly say I disliked the listening-post duty that first time. Nothing happened of course. There was no killing, but it was nervy work. Later, in common with other fellows, I was able to go on listening-post with the same nonchalance as my first coster friend. It lies in whether one is used to the thing or not. Nothing comes easy at first, especially in the trenches. Later on, it is all in the day's work.

When our relief came we crawled back to our trench and spent the night in our dugouts. Next day we got a change of rations. We had "Maconochie." "He" is by way of a stew. Stew with a tin jacket. It bears the nomenclature of its inventor and maker, although Maconochie's is a firm. This is an English ration and after bully beef for weeks, it is a pleasant enough change.

The weather was fine: clear overhead, blue sky and just a hint of frost, though it was not very cold. After dinner the first day in the trenches, I suddenly noticed an excitement among the English soldiers. We became excited, too, and strained to see what was happening.

There, sheer ahead of us, darting, twisting, turning, was a monoplane right over the German trench. It was a British plane, and taking inconceivably risky chances. We could see the airman on the steering seat wave to us. He seemed like a gigantic mosquito, bent on tormenting the Huns. Their bullets spurted round him. He spiraled and sank, sank and spiraled. Nothing ever hit him. The Boches got wildly hysterical in their shooting. Every rifle pointed upward. They forgot where they were; they forgot us; they fired rapidly, round after round. And still the plane rose and fell, flitted higher and looped lower. It was a magnificent display. We could see the aviator wave more clearly now; his broad smile almost made us imagine we heard his exultant laugh.

"Who is it? What is it?" We boys gasped out the questions breathlessly.

"'Ere he comes; watch 'im, mate; watch 'im. 'E's the Mad Major. Look, look—he's looping! Gawd in 'eaven, they've got 'im. No, blimey, 'e's blinkin' luck itself. 'E's up again."

"Who is the Mad Major?" I asked, but got no answer. Every eye was on the wild career of the plane.

The Germans got more reckless. They stood in their trenches. We fired. We got them by the ones and twos. They ducked, then—swoop—again the major was over them, and again they forgot. Up went their rifles, and spatter, spatter, the bullets went singing upward.

It was about an hour after that we heard a voice cry down to us: "Cheer up, boys, all's well." There, overhead, was the Mad Major in his plane. Elusive as was the elusive Pimpernel, he flitted back of the lines to the plane-base.

"Who is he?" We crowded round the English Tommies when all was quiet.

"The Mad Major, Canuck," they answered. "The Mad Major."

"Yes, but—"

"Never 'eard of 'im, 'ave yer?" It was a sergeant who spoke, and we closed round, thinking to hear a tale.

"'E comes round 'ere every evenin', 'e does. 'E 'as no fear, that chap, 'e 'asn't. Does it to cheer us up. Didn't yer 'ear 'im as 'e went? 'E 'arries them, 'e does, 'arries them proper. Down 'e'll go, up 'e'll go, and ne'er a bullet within singing distance of 'im. 'E's steeped in elusion!" The sergeant finished, proud of having found a phrase, no matter what might be its true meaning, that illustrated what he wished to convey.

The Mad Major certainly appeared immune from all of the enemy's fire.

The sergeant went on. He, himself, had been with the Imperial forces since August, 1914. He had fought through the Aisne, the Marne, and the awful retreat from Mons.

'Twas at Mons, he told us, that the Mad Major earned his sobriquet, and first showed his daring. During those awful black days when slowly, slowly and horribly, French and British and Belgians fought a backward fight, day after day and hour after hour, losing now a yard, now a mile, but always going back—then it was that with the dreadful weight of superior numbers—maybe twenty to one—the Germans had a chance to win. Then it was they lost, and lost for all time.

All through this rearguard action there was the Mad Major. Mounted on his airy steed, he flitted above the clouds, below the clouds. Sometimes swallowed in the smoke of the enemy's big guns; sometimes diving to avoid a shell; sometimes staggering as though wounded, but always righting himself. There would be the Mad Major each day, over the rearguard troops, seeming to shelter them. He would harry the German line; he would drop a bomb, flit back, and with a brave "We've got them, boys," cheer the sinking spirits of the wearied foot soldiers.

The Mad Major was a wonder. Every part of the line he visited, and was known the length and breadth of the Allied armies.

Though for the moment the Mad Major had disappeared from our view, we were to hear more of him later on.

CHAPTER VII

WHO STARTED THE WAR?

The wisest thing that our commanders did was to sandwich the Canadian boys in with the British regulars. Without a doubt we of the First Division were the greenest troops that ever landed in France.

In two short turns that we spent with the British, we learned more than we could have otherwise in a month's training. We also became inspired with that "Keep cool and crack a joke" spirit that is so splendidly Anglo-Saxon.

I am not an Englishman, and I did not think very much of an Englishman before going overseas. I regarded him more or less as not "worth while." It did not take a year to convince me that the Englishman is very much "worth while."

The English soldier chums up quickly. The traditional formality and conventionality of the English are traditions only. There is none of it in the trenches.

Discipline there is, strict discipline, among men and officers. Between officer and man there is a marked respect, and a marked good fellowship which never degenerates into familiarity.

There is love between the English officer and the English soldier. A love that has been proved many times, when the commissioned man has sacrificed his life to save the man of lower rank; when the private has crossed the pathway of hell itself to save a fallen leader.

The English soldier, and when I say English I mean to include Welsh, Scotch and Irish, reserves to himself the right to "grouse." He grouses at everything great or small which has no immediate or vital bearing on the situation. As soon as anything arises that would really warrant a grouse—napoo! Tommy Atkins then begins to smile. He grouses when he has to clean his buttons; he grouses loudly and fiercely when a puttee frays to rags, and he grouses when his tea is too hot.

But when Tommy runs out of ammunition, is partly surrounded by the enemy, is almost paralyzed by bombardment; when he is literally in the last ditch, with a strip of cold steel the only thing between him and death—then Tommy smiles, then he cracks a joke. Without a thought of himself, without a murmur, he faces any desperate plight.

He smiles as he rattles his last bullet into place; he grins as his bayonet snaps from the hilt, and he goes to it hand-to-hand with doubled fists, a tag of a song on his lips, for "Death or Glory."

That is Tommy Atkins as I saw him. That is the real Britisher of the Old Country. We shall know him from now on in his true light, and the knowledge will make for a better understanding among the peoples of the English-speaking world.

It was Sandy Clark who, eating a hunch of bread and bully beef in a dugout, got partly buried when an H.E. (high explosive) came over. Sandy crawled out unhurt, his sandwich somewhat muddy but intact, and made his way down the trench to a clear space. Here he sat down beside a sentry, finished his bully beef and muddy bread, wiped his mouth, and remarked some ten minutes after the explosion: "That was a close one."

Imperturbable under danger; certain of his own immediate immunity from death; confident of his regiment's invincibility; with a deep-rooted love of home and an unalterable belief in the might and right of Britain—there is Tommy Atkins.

Looking back from the vantage point of nearly two years, it seems to me that we were somewhat like young unbroken colts. We were restless and untrained, with an overplus of spirits difficult to control. Gradually the English Tommy influenced us until we gained much of his steadiness of purpose, his bulldog tenacity and his insouciance.

Tommy never instructed us by word of mouth. He lived his creed in his daily rounds. He never knows that he is beaten, therefore a beating is never his. We have gained the same outlook, simply by association with him.

Were I a general and had I a position to *take*, I would choose soldiers of one nation as quickly as another—French, Australians, Africans, Indians, Americans or Canadians. Were I a general and had I a position to *retain*, to hold against all odds, then, without a moment's hesitation, I would send English troops and English troops only.

Now and again an American or a Canadian newspaper would come our way. "Anything to read" is a never-ending cry at the front, and every scrap of newspaper is read, discussed and read again. In the early days of 1914-15, these newspapers would have long and weighty editorials which called forth longer and weightier letters from "veritas" and "old subscriber." We boys read those editorials and letters, and wondered;

wondered how sane men could waste time in writing such stuff, how sane men could set it in type and print it, and more than all we wondered how sane men could read it. "Who started the war?" they asked.

"Bah!" we would say to one another, "who started the war? If only those folks who write and print and read such piffle, no matter what their nationality, could have had five minutes' look at the German trenches and another five minutes' look at the French and British trenches—never again would they query, 'Who started the war?'"

We of the Allied army knew nothing of trench warfare. After the fierce onslaught on Paris, which failed, the Germans entrenched. Thank God, they did. They entrenched, and by entrenching they have won the war for us. They made a mistake then that they can never now retrieve.

They were in a position to choose, and they chose to entrench in the high dry sections, leaving the low-lying swamps, the damp marshy lands, for us. We had no alternative. It was either to take a stand there on what footing was left or be wiped off the map. We stood.

On that sector between La Bassee and Armentières it was practically an impossibility to dig in. The muddy water was of inconceivable thickness along the greater length of the whole front. It oused and eddied, it seemed to swirl and draw as though there were a tide. We did not attempt to dig. We raised sandbag breastworks some five or six feet high and lay behind them day in and day out for an eternity, as it seemed.

Our shift in the trenches was supposed to be four days and four nights in. It never was shorter, sometimes much longer. Once we spent eleven days and nights in the trenches without a shift, because our reinforcing battalion was called away to another sector of the front. I know of a Highland Battalion that was in twenty-eight days and nights without a change.

We were unequipped as to uniform. We were in the regulation khaki of other days. We had no waterproof overcoats. We had puttees, but the greater number of us had no rubber boots. A very few of the men had boots of rubber that reached to the knees. At first we envied the possessors of these, but not for long. The water and mud, and shortly the blood, rose above the top and ran down inside the leg of the boot. The wearers could not remove the mud, and trench feet, frost bite, gangrene, was their immediate portion. We lost as many men, that first winter of the war, by these terrible afflictions as we did by actual bullets and shell fire.

To us who had come from the Far Northwest the weather was a terrible trial. Our winters were possibly more severe, but we could stand them so much better, with their sharp dry cold in contrast to the damp, misty, soaking chill of this non-zero country. Possibly, at night, the thermometer would register some two or three degrees below freezing. A thin shell of ice would form on the ditch which we called a trench. This would crackle round our legs and the cold would eat into the very bone. At dawn the ice would begin to break up and a steady sleet begin to fall. Later the sleet would turn to rain, and so the day would pass till we were soaked through to the skin. At night the frost would come again and stiffen our clothes to our tortured bodies, next day another thaw and rain, and so to the end of our turn, or to the time when an enemy bullet would finish our physical suffering.

We could have borne all this without a murmur, and did bear it in a silence that was grim, but we had a greater strain, a mental one, with which to contend. We knew—we knew without a doubt that we were out there alone. We had not a reserve behind us. We had not a tithe of the gun power which we should have had. Our artillery was not appreciable in quantity. What there was of it was effective, but as compared to the enemy gun power we were nowhere. They had possibly ten to our one. They were very considerably stronger than they are to-day. We, to-day, can say with truth that we are where they were in 1914-15. We, with our two years of hurried and almost frenzied work, and they, with their forty years of crafty preparation!

And they knew how to use those guns, too. Our engineering and pioneer corps at that time were non-existent. We had practically none. The Germans would put over a few shells during the day. They would level our sandbag breastworks and blow our frail shelters to smithereens. We had no dugouts and no communication trenches. With a shell of tremendous power they would rip up yards of our makeshift defenses and kill half a dozen of our boys. Sometimes we would groan aloud and pray to see a few German legs and arms fly to the four winds as compensation. But no. We would wire back to artillery headquarters: "For God's sake, send over a few shells, even one shell, to silence this hell!" And day after day the same answer would come back: "Heaven knows we are sorry, but you've had your allotment of shells for to-day."

Perhaps one shell, or it may have been three, would have been the ammunition ration of our particular front for the day.

It was nobody's fault at the moment of fighting. It lay perhaps between those who had anticipated and prepared for war for forty years and those who had neglected to foresee the possibility of such an enterprise. The fact remained, we had no shells.

Every day our defenses were leveled. Every night we would crawl out, after long hours spent flat on our stomachs, covered to the neck in mud and blood, and endeavor to repair the damage. Every night we lost a few men; every day we lost a few men, and still we held our ground.

The day casualties were the worst. The wounded men had to lie in the damp and dirt until night came to shelter them; then some one would help, or if that were not possible, the wounded would have to make his own pain-strewn way back to a dressing station. During the day some one might discover that he had developed a frozen toe. He could get no relief; he dare not attempt to leave his partial shelter. The slightest movement, and the enemy would have closed his career. By night his foot would be a fiery torture, and by the time a doctor was near enough to help it would be a rotting mass of gangrene, and one man more would be added to the list of permanent cripples.

I am asked, "How did you live? How did you 'carry on'?"

Many a time I have said to myself in thinking of the enemy: "Why don't they come on—why don't the fools strike now? There's no earthly reason why they should not defeat us, and roll on triumphantly to Paris, to Calais, to London, to New York, and so realize their original intention." There was no *earthly* reason. No.

The Kaiser had talked in lordly voice of "ME and God." The Kaiser has manufactured a God of his own fancy, a God of blood and iron. There is no such God for us. For us, there was always that Unseen Hand which held back the enemy in his might. The All Highest who is not on the side of blood and murder and pillage and outrage and violation; the Almighty, who, crudely though I may express it, is with those who fight for the Right and on the square.

And that is why we were not driven back to the sea. That is why we stood the test. That is why we, the Allied Nations, shall win.

Again, if the German hordes, with their iron power behind them, had had five per cent. of the Anglo-Saxon sporting blood in their veins, they could have licked us long ago. They did not. They have not. They are poor sports. They have eliminated the individuality of "sport" for the efficiency of machinery, and they can not lick us.

Who started the war? The War Machine that had the preparation of half a century, or the peace-loving peoples who, at a day's notice, took their stand for humanity?

Who started the war? There is no room for argument. The Germans started the war.

Who will finish the war? There is no room or argument. We will finish the war.

CHAPTER VIII

"AND OUT OF EVIL THERE SHALL COME THAT WHICH IS GOOD"

The worst days of this war are over. The worst days were those through which we came in the winter of 1914-15. The war may last ten years; the war may be over inside of a few months. Neither contingency would surprise me. We might lose twice as many in killed and wounded as we did through that winter; every white man, British, French, American, of military age, might pay the supreme price, and yet the worst days are gone by.

The worst days of the war passed when the chance of the Hun defeating us was lost. Though all the flower of our manhood were crippled or dead, though our old men and our boys were called to the field, though women had to gird on sword and buckler, none of these things could be worse than to be licked—licked is the word—by a dastardly and cowardly foe.

And if the German Army at the zenith of its strength could not lick one thin line of English, of French and Canadians, how can they lick us when we have Uncle Sam in the balance?

A question to daunt even the scientific brain of a Kaiser, of a Hindenburg, of a Von Bernstorff.

The folks back home are always wondering and inquiring how it is possible to feed the troops under such terrible and awful conditions. The folks back home are the only ones who worry. We do not. Tommy Atkins is much more sure of getting his rations to-morrow than he is of living until to-morrow to eat them.

Right here I would pay a sincere tribute to two departments of our British Army. The Commissary Department which supplies every want of the soldier, from a high explosive shell to a button. It is as near to the one hundred per cent. mark of efficiency as it is possible for a human organization to become. It is not too much to say that it is perfect.

The other department is that of the Medical Corps, the R.A.M.C., or the Red Cross. It is all the same. It is all run with the precision of clockwork. Its whole aim for the comfort and succor of Tommy. Of this department I speak in a later chapter.

The food for the millions of men in France is concentrated at what we may call the Great Base, and from there it is distributed to the different army corps. In each army corps there are two or more divisions. In a division there are three infantry and three artillery brigades, three field companies of engineers, three field ambulances and details. In each infantry brigade are four battalions and in each artillery four batteries. To one company are four platoons, and about seventy men to a platoon.

Each body of men as I have named them is really a separate and distinct unit in itself, but cooperating with all others. The food from the base is brought to the army corps by rail, and is distributed to the divisional headquarters by divisional transports which are operated by the Army Service Corps or the Mechanical Transport. From the divisional headquarters the next step is to the brigades, and brigade transports collect the food and take it another few miles nearer to the boys.

Battalion transport wagons then bring the food and other supplies down to battalion headquarters. At these headquarters are the quartermaster sergeants of each company, and they, with their staff, during the daytime pack up and get ready for distribution supplies for each separate platoon. At night the company wagons, already packed, are drawn up as close to the trenches as conditions will permit. If the country is too torn with shells to permit the use of horses, men will drag them.

I have seen these wagons sometimes within five hundred yards of the front line trenches, and again ration parties may have to crawl back a mile before meeting them. It all depends on a number of circumstances. On a moonlight night it is not possible to come so close as on a dark night. In rain the wagons may sink into mud-holes, or in badly shelled areas there is danger of their turning over into a hole. Everything depends on conditions and the good judgment of the man in charge.

©Famous Players—Lasky Corporation. Scene from the Photo-Play THE HUN COMES TO TOWN.

Each evening from each section, and there are four sections to a platoon, the corporal or sergeant in command will detail a couple of men for ration party. Ration party is no pleasant job; as Tommy terms it, it is "one of the rottenest ever."

©Famous Players—Lasky Corporation. Scene from the Photo-Play "WHO'S THE GIRL, PEAT?"

The two unhappy boys will crawl out as soon as it is dark. They reach the supply wagon, or it may be only a dump of goods. There they will find the quartermaster in charge, in all likelihood. To him they tell their platoon number—Number Sixteen Platoon, Section Four, perhaps—and the quartermaster will hand them the rations. One man will get half a dozen parcels, maybe more. His comrade never offers to relieve him of any—to the comrade there is designated a higher duty. The quartermaster takes up with care and hands with tenderness to the second man a jar, or possibly a jug.

On going back to the trenches a thoughtless sentry may halt the ration party. I have seen it done. I have heard the conversation. I dare not write it. There goes one of the boys, both arms hugging a miscellaneous assortment of packages. He slips and struggles and swears and falls, then picks himself up and gathers together the scattered bundles. But what of the other? A jug held tightly in both hands, he chooses his steps as would a dainty Coryphee. He dare not trip. He dare not fall. He MUST not spill one drop. Jugs are hard to replace in France; in fact, it is much easier to get a jug in Nebraska than in France.

The boys finally reach the trench in safety, and next morning the rations are issued at "stand-to." "Stand-to" is the name given to the sunrise hour, and again that hour at night when every man stands to the parapet in full equipment and with fixed bayonet. After morning stand-to bayonets are unfixed, for if the sunlight should glint upon the polished steel our position might be disclosed to some sniper.

To my mind stand-to is more or less a relic of the early days of the war, when these two hours were those most favored by the Germans for attack, and so it has become a custom to be in readiness.

A day's rations in the trenches consists of quite a variety of commodities. First thing in the winter morning we have that controversial blind, rum. We get a "tot" which is about equal to a tablespoonful. It is not compulsory, and no man need take it unless he wishes. This is not the time or place to discuss the temperance question, but our commanders and the army surgeons believe that rum as a medicine, as a stimulant, is necessary to the health of the soldier, therefore the rum is issued.

We take this ration as a prescription. We gulp it down when half frozen, and nearly paralyzed after standing a night in mud and blood and ice, often to the waistline, rarely below the ankle, and it revives us as tea, cocoa or coffee could never do. We are not made drunkards by our rum ration. The great majority of us have never tasted medicinal rum before reaching the trenches; there is a rare chance that any of us will ever taste it, or want to taste it, again after leaving the trenches.

The arguments against rum make Mr. Tommy Atkins tired, and I may say in passing that I have never yet seen a chaplain refuse his ration. And of the salt of the good God's earth are the chaplains. There was Major the Reverend John Pringle, of Yukon fame, whose only son Jack was killed in action after he had walked two hundred miles to enlist. No cant, no smug psalm-singing, mourners'-bench stuff for him. He believed in his Christianity like a man; he was ready to fight for his belief like a man; he cared for us like a father, and stood beside us in the mornings as we drank our stimulant. Again, I repeat if a man is found drunk while on active service, he is liable to court martial and death. A few years' training of this kind will make the biggest pre-war drunkard come back home a sober man.

Each soldier carries into the trenches with him sufficient coke and wood to last for his four days in. Upon the brazier he cooks his own meals. For the first few months we were unable to place our braziers on the ground; they would have sunk into the mud. If we attempted to cook anything we would stick a bayonet into a sandbag and hang the brazier on it, then cook in our mess tins over that.

To-day there are dugouts, trench platforms and other conveniences which simplify the domestic arrangements of the trenches to a marvelous degree.

A soldier is at liberty to cook his own rations by himself, but as a rule we all chum in together. We may all take a hand in the cooking, or we may appoint a section cook for a day or for a week, according to his especial facility.

After the rum ration we receive some tea and sugar, lots of bully beef and biscuits. The bully beef is corned beef and has its origin, mysterious to us, in Chicago, Illinois, or so we believe. It is quite good. But you can get too much of a good thing once too often. So sometimes we eat it, and sometimes we use the unopened tins as bricks and line the trenches with them. Good solid bricks, too! We get soup powders and yet more soup powders. We get cheese that is not cream cheese, and we get a slice of raw bacon. Often we eat the bacon at once, sometimes we save it up to have a "good feed" at one time. One can plan one's own menu just as fancy dictates.

Then we get jam. The inevitable, haunting, horrific "plum and apple." This is made by Ticklers', Limited, of London, England, and after the tins are empty we use them to manufacture hand grenades. In those days our supply of hand bombs was like our supply of shells, problematic to say the least. After a time, back of the line, instruction schools were opened in bomb making and bomb throwing. One or two out of a platoon would go back and learn "how," and then instruct the rest of us to fill the tins with spent pieces of shrapnel, old scraps of iron, anything which came handy, insert the fuse, cotton and so forth, and thus form an effective weapon for close fighting.

We called those bombers "Ticklers' Artillery Brigade," and they tickled many a German with Ticklers' empty jam tins.

A stock of weak tea, some sugar, salt, some bully beef, biscuits crumbled down, the whole well stirred and brought to a boil, then thickened by several soup powders, is a recipe for a stew which, as the Irishman said, is "filling and feeding." Of its appearance I say nothing.

Regardless of any, we are the best fed troops in the field. While in the trenches the food may be rough and monotonous, but there is plenty of it, and it is of the best quality of its kind. No man need ever be hungry in the trenches. It is his own fault if he is.

We grouse at our rations, of course, and make jokes and laugh, but we never run short of supplies.

Behind the lines, when we go back for a rest and are in billets, we are supplied with well-cooked and comfortable meals. Three good squares a day. We have here our field kitchens and our regular cooks, and Mulligan (stew) is not the daily portion, but variations of roast beef, mutton and so forth.

It is good food, and I have heard men exclaim that it was better than anything they had had at home. After investigation I usually found that the men who dilated thus on the gastronomic delights of billets were married men!

The authorities are just as careful about sending up a soldier's letters, his parcels and small gifts from home, as they are about the food and clothing supplies. They recognize that Tommy Atkins naturally and rightly wants to keep in touch with the home folks, and every effort is made to get communications up on time. But war is war, and there are days and even weeks when no letters reach the front line. Those are the days that try the mettle of the men. We do not tell our thoughts to one another. The soldier of to-day is rough of exterior, rough of speech and rough of bearing, but underneath he has a heart of gold and a spirit of untold gentleness.

We play poker, and we play with the sky the limit. Why not? Active service allowance is thirty francs a month—five dollars. Why put on any limit? You may owe a man a hundred, or even two hundred dollars, but what's the difference?—a shell may put an end to you, him and the poker board any old minute. There is no knowing.

Weeks pass and no letters. We play more wildly, squatting down in the mud with the board before us. I have sometimes seen a full house, a straight, three of a kind, or probably four big ones. "I raise you five," says Bill. Bang!—a whiz bang explodes twenty yards away. "I raise you ten." Bang!—a wee willie takes the top off the parapet. "There's your ten, and ten better." Crash!—and several bits of shrapnel probably go through the board. "You're called. Gee, but that was a close one! Deal 'em out, Peat."

Suddenly down the trench will pass the word that the officer and sergeant are coming with letters and parcels. We kick the poker board high above the trench, cards and chips flying in all directions. No one cares, even though he's had a hand full of aces. The letters are in, and every man is dead sure there will be one for him.

We crowd around the officer with shining eyes like so many schoolboys. Parcels are handed out first, but we throw these aside to be opened later, and snatch for the letters. But luck is not always good to all of us, and possibly it will be old Bill who has to turn away empty-handed and alone. No letter. Are they all well, or—no letter.

But Bill is not left alone very long. A pal will notice him, notice him before he himself has had more than a glimpse of the heading of his own precious letter, and going over to Bill, will slap him a hearty blow on the shoulder and say: "Say, Bill, old boy, I've got a letter. Listen to this—" And then, no matter how sacred the letter may be, he will read it aloud before he has a chance to glance at it himself. If it is from the girl, old Bill will be laughing before it is finished—girls write such amusing stuff; but, no matter whom it is from, it is all the same. It is a pleasure shared, and Bill forgets his trouble in the happiness of another.

Kindness, unselfishness and sympathy are all engendered by trench life. There is no school on earth to equal the school of generous thoughtfulness which is found on the battle-fields of Europe to-day. There we men are finding ourselves in that we are finding true sympathy with our brother man. We have everything in common. We have the hardship of the trench, and the nearness of death. The man of title, the Bachelor of Arts, the bootblack, the lumberjack and the millionaire's son meet on common ground. We wear the same uniform, we think the same thoughts, we do not remember what we were, we only know what we are—soldiers fighting in the same great cause.

CHAPTER IX

ALL FUSSED UP AND NO PLACE TO GO

Some days in the trenches are dreariness itself. Sometimes we get discouraged to the point of exhaustion, but these days are rare and when they do occur there is always an alleviation. In every trench, in every section, there is some one who is a joker; who is a true humorist, and who can carry the spirits of the troops with him to the place where grim reality vanishes and troubles are forgotten.

The nights pass quickly enough because at night we have plenty to do. But even while carrying out duties at night many humorous things happen. Take, for instance, the passing of messages up and down the line.

To the civilian message-sending might appear much the same day or night, but not so. In the day we can speak without fear of being overheard, but at night no one knows but that Hans or Fritz may be a few feet on the other side of the parapet with ears cocked for all sounds. So communications have to be made with care. Sometimes the change of a syllable might alter the meaning of a sentence and cause disaster.

A message at night is whispered in lowest tones from man to man. This is a branch of the service for the young recruit to practise. It means much, and a thoughtless error is unpardonable. The first man receives the communication from the officer. Through the silence will come a soft "Hs-s-s." The next in line will creep up and get the words. He in turn calls to the next man and whispers on the order.

It was one night early in the fighting that Major Kirkpatrick sent the message down the line four hundred yards along: "Major Kirkpatrick says to tell Captain Parkes to send up reinforcements to the right in a hurry." That was the message as I got it. That was the message as I transmitted it to the next man. To Captain Parkes the message ran in a hurried whisper: "Major Kirkpatrick says to tell Captain Parkes to send up 'three and fourpence' to the right in a hurry."

When Major Kirkpatrick received three shillings and fourpence he was almost in a state of collapse. Luckily, the situation was not serious, or possibly we might have lost heavily. This shows how imperative it is to have absolute accuracy.

Again, at nights there are different kinds of raids to be carried out. Probably a raid by wire cutters, or possibly an actual trench raid. Nights in France are not meant for sleep. There is usually one hour on duty and two hours off, and something doing all the while.

But the days frequently grow long and tiresome. We sleep, we tell stories, we read when there is anything to read, and we write letters if we have the materials. Or, above all, we work out some new device to spring upon the Boche.

In the early days of the war we knew nothing about hand grenades. The Germans started to use them on us, but it was not a great while before we fell into line and produced bombs to match theirs. At first we had the Tickler variety as previously described; since then we have used the "hair-brush" and others, but to-day we are using the standardized Mill hand grenade.

I can never forget the first bomb that was thrown from our trench. Volunteers were asked for this new and risky job. I will not mention the name of the boy who volunteered in our section, but he was a big, hefty, red-haired chap. He has since been killed. It is noticeable that red-haired fellows are impetuous and frequently ahead of others in bravery, for a moment or two, anyway.

That day there was an additional supply of mud and water in our trench. We were dragging around in it until the bombing commenced, then we crowded like boys round the big fellow, who was close to the parapet, his chest stuck out, his voice vibrant with pride as he said, "Just you wait and see me blow those fellows to smithereens—just you wait and see!"

In those days of makeshift bombs there was a nine-second fuse in each. We were about thirty yards from the Germans' trench. Of course it would not take nine seconds for the bomb to travel thirty yards; rather would it arrive in three seconds, and give Hans and Fritz opportunity to pick it up comfortably and return it in time for its explosion to kill us and not them. Thus the order was to count at least five—one, two, three, four, five—slowly and carefully, after the fuse was lighted and before the bomb left the hand.

Every one had his eyes glued to the periscope, except myself. I watched the fuse in the hand of that red-haired guy. He started to count—one, two, and his hand began to shake; at three his hand was moving about violently; at four the bomb fell. I wonder if there is any one in the world who thinks that we stopped there to see that bomb explode. No, we didn't.

There was a chance right there for the quick thinker, for the man of extraordinary initiative, to win the V.C.

Somehow our initiative took us in the other direction. It is really wonderful how fast the average man can beat it when he knows there is certain death should he linger in one spot very long. The way we traveled round the traverse and up the trenches was not slow.

Usually there is something going on, but there are days when a man would not think there was a war at all. It is not every day at the front that both sides are shelling and strafing. We once faced a certain Saxon regiment and for nearly two weeks neither side fired a bullet. This particular Saxon regiment said to us: "We are Saxons, you are Anglo-Saxons, we are not a bit fussy about shooting as long as you won't." So, as our turns came periodically, we faced them and did not shoot.

Actually we sent out working parties in the daytime, both Saxon and British, but such things do not happen any more. And such a situation never yet happened with a Prussian or Bavarian regiment. Those devils like to shoot for the sake of hearing their rifles go off.

There are days, when fighting at close quarters, that both sides feel pretty good. The morning will be bright, and we may open the proceedings by trying to sing German songs, and they will join in by singing British airs, but always in a sarcastic manner, after putting words to them that I dare not write.

On the first day of July, which is Dominion or Confederation Day, the Germans began by singing to a certain Eastern Canadian regiment the first verse of our national anthem, *O! Canada.* When they got through, they politely asked the young braves of this regiment to sing the second verse. The Canadian boys sent over a few bombs instead, for they did not know the words of the second verse! Not to know the second verse seems to be one of the idiosyncrasies of the peoples of all nations, bar the German!

Should we get tired of singing, we would shout across to the enemy trenches. We would ask pertinent questions about their commanders and impertinent ones about the affairs of their nation. One thing I can say for Hans—he is never slow in answering. His repartee may be clumsy, but it is prompt and usually effective.

We would inquire after the health of old "Von Woodenburg," old "One O'clock," the "Clown Prince," or "One Bumstuff." Hans would take this in a jocular way, slamming back something about Sir Wilfrid Laurier, Lloyd George, or Sir Sham Shoes, but when we really wanted to get Fritz's goat we would tease him about the Kaiser.

We would shout "*Gott strafe der Kaiser!*" That would put them up in the air higher than a balloon. We would feel like getting out and hitting one another, but we dare not even raise a finger because a sniper would take it off. But after a lull there is always a storm, so before many minutes a bullet would go "crack," which would be the signal for thousands of rifles on both sides to commence an incessant firing. All this over nothing, and nobody getting hurt.

It put me in mind of a couple of old women scrapping over a back-yard fence, and as we say back home, "all fussed up and no place to go."

CHAPTER X

HELLO! SKY-PILOT!

At the outset of the war there was much speculation as to the response the Lion's cubs would make to the call for help. Britain, herself, never doubted that her children, now fully grown and very strong, would rally to the old flag as in the earlier days of their greater dependency. But Britain, England, is of the Brer Rabbit type—she sits still and says nuffin'.

The neutrals speculated on the attitude of Canada. German propaganda had been busy, and certain sections of the Canadian public had been heard to say that they had no part with England—but that was before the war. The speculative neutral had a shock and a disappointment. Not a Canadian, man or woman, but remembered that England was "home," and home was threatened. As one man they answered the short sharp cry.

Australia, New Zealand and South Africa provided food for conversation among the nations then not engaged in the fight. South Africa had a rising, fostered by German money and German lies, but it fizzled out before the determined attitude, not of England, but of the men who counted in South Africa itself. All of these countries, which used to be colonies, came without question when the need arose. They may have had minor disagreements with the Old Country, they may have resented the last lingering parental attitude of the Motherland, but let any one touch as an enemy that Motherland and that enemy had well have cried, "Peccavi!" on the moment.

Above all, the neutrals wondered about India. That vast Far Eastern Empire with her millions of men—what would India do?

What did India do? The maharajahs threw into the coffers of the homeland millions of money, they threw in jewels in quantity to be judged by weight of hundreds, in value to be judged in millions of pounds. They offered their men and their lahks of rupees without reservation. The regular troops of the Eastern Empire, the Ghurkas, the Pathans, the Sikhs, a half dozen others, clamored to be taken over to Europe to fight at the front for the great White Chief.

The Indian troops came to Europe, landed in France, and took up their stand on the western front. To them I must make special reference. Some idea may be abroad that because the Hindu troops are not still in France that they proved poor fighters. This is very far from the truth. The Indian regiments were among our best, but they could not stand the rigors of the European climate. They had been used to the warmth and brightness and dryness of their homeland; they came to cold and rain and mud and unknown discomforts. It was too much. Again, the Indian is made for open, hand-to-hand warfare. Give him a hill to climb and hold, give him a forest to crawl through and gain his point, give him open land to pass over without being seen, he can not be beaten. But the strain, mental and physical, of trench life was too much.

To the Indian, war is a religion. One day I went down the line to where a body of Ghurkas were lying to our left. I walked along about a mile through the muddy ditches and at last came up with one of the men. I stopped and spoke, then offered him a fag. After this interchange of courtesies we fell into conversation. He did not know very much English, and I no Hindustani at all, but in a short time one of the Ghurka officers approached. The officers and men of these regiments are very friendly, more chummy almost than are our officers to our men. This officer acted as an interpreter, and together they told me much that I was anxious to know.

After a little I asked the Ghurka to show me his knife, but he would not. The Ghurka knife is a weapon of wonderful grace. It is short and sharpened on both edges, while it is broad and curved almost to the angle of a sickle. It is used in a flat sweeping movement, which, when wielded by an expert, severs a limb or a head at one blow. I was told that at twenty yards, when they throw it, they never miss.

At last, through the agency of the officer, I found that it is against all the laws of battle for a soldier of this clan to remove his knife from the scabbard unless he draws blood with the naked blade. The unfailing courtesy of the Hindu forbade a continued refusal, and as I urged him the soldier at last slowly drew the blade from its sheath. He did not raise it for me to examine, nor did he lift his eyes to mine until he had pricked his hand between the thumb and first finger and raised a jet of his own red blood. Then only did I have the privilege of looking at his treasured weapon.

The Hindu warrior believes that to die in battle is to win at once a coveted eternity in Erewohne. He does not wish to be merely wounded, he desires death in fight rather than immunity from injury. He does not evade danger; rather he seeks it.

Shortly after this, at the great battle of Neuve Chapelle, where the British took over five miles of trenches and four miles of front from the enemy, the Hindu troops distinguished themselves in magnificent charges. They leaped out of the trenches almost before the word of command had reached their hearing. Fleet of foot and lithe of action, they had sprung into the enemy trenches and slashed the Hun to submission before the heavier white men had got across the intervening country. They were wonderful, full of dash and courage, but the difficulties of the situation called for an alteration of their fighting *milieu*.

Feeding these troops also was a matter of considerable moment. Their religion forbade the eating of any meat but that of the goat. These animals must be freshly killed and must be killed by the Hindu himself. This entailed the bringing up to the line of herds of live goats. In addition, many other formalities of food supply had to be taken into account.

With the most fervent thanks for the good work done on our western front, the authorities came to the conclusion that our cousins of the East would be even greater in service on one of our other fronts. They have gone since to Egypt, to Saloniki, to Mesopotamia, and to the East and West African fronts. They are playing a magnificent and unforgetable part in the world war. They have endeared themselves to the hearts of the folks at home and they have earned the lasting gratitude of all of us. They have defended their section of the empire as we have defended our northern part of the red splotches which mark Britain on the map.

I was sorry that the Indian regiments had to be removed from the west front, because, undoubtedly, they were the most feared by the Hun. The Indian was at his best in a charge, but at night he had an uneasy habit of crawling out of the trench toward Fritz, with his knife held firmly between his teeth. Before dawn he would return, his knife still in his teeth, but in his hand a German head.

To-day the Canadians in France are known by the enemy as the "white Ghurkas," and this, to us, is one of the highest compliments. The Ghurkas are considered bravest of the brave. Shall we not be proud to share a title such as this?

As the religion of the Ghurka follows him to the battle-field, so in a different sense does the religion of the white man. We have our thoughts, our hopes and our aspirations. Some of us have our Bibles and our prayer-books, some of us have rosaries and crucifixes. All of us have deep in our hearts love, veneration and respect for the sky-pilot—chaplain, if you would rather call him so.

To us sky-pilot, and very truly so, the man who not only points the way to higher things, but the man who travels with us over the rough road which leads to peace in our innermost selves.

It does not matter of what sect or of what denomination these men may be. Out on the battle-field there are Anglican clergy, there are Roman Catholic priests, there are ministers of the Presbyterian, the Methodist, the Baptist and other non-conformist faiths. Creed and doctrine play no part when men are gasping out a dying breath and the last message home. The chaplain carries in his heart the comfort for the man who is facing eternity. We do not want to die. We are all strong and full of life and hope and power of doing. Suddenly we are stricken beyond mortal aid. The chaplain comes and in a few phrases gives us the password, the sign which admits us to the peaceful Masonry of Christianity. Rough men pass away, hard men "go West" with a smile of peace upon their pain-tortured lips if the padre can get to them in time for the parting word, the cheerful, colloquial "best o' luck."

Does the padre come to us and sanctimoniously pronounce our eternal doom should he hear us swear? The clergyman, the minister of old time, is down and out when he reaches the battle-fields of France, or any other of the fronts we are holding. No stupid tracts are handed to us, no whining and groaning, no morbid comments on the possibility of eternal damnation. No, the chaplain of to-day is a real man, maybe he always was, I don't know. A man who risks his life as do we who are in the fighting line. He has services, talks, addresses, but he never preaches. He practises all the time.

Out of this war there will come a new religion. It won't be a sin any more to sing rag-time on Sunday, as it was in the days of my childhood. It won't be a sin to play a game on Sunday. After church parade in France we rushed to the playing fields behind the lines, and many a time I've seen the chaplain umpire the ball game. Many a time I've seen him take a hand in a friendly game of poker. The man who goes to France to-day will come back with a broadened mind, be he a chaplain or be he a fighter. There is no room for narrowness, for dogma or for the tenets of old-time theology. This is a man-size business, and in every department men are meeting the situation as real men should.

Again, at Neuve Chapelle, there was magnificent bravery. Just across the street, at a turn, there lay a number of wounded men. They were absolutely beyond the reach of succor. A terrible machine gun fire swept the roadway between them and a shelter of sandbags, which had hastily been put up on one side of the street. By these sandbags a sergeant had been placed on guard with strictest orders to forbid the passing of any one, without exception, toward the area where the wounded lay. It was certain death to permit it. We had no men to spare, we had no men to lose, we had to conserve every one of our effectives.

As time wore on and the enemy fire grew hotter, a Roman Catholic chaplain reached the side of the sergeant. "Sergeant, I want to go over to the aid of those wounded men."

"No, sir, my orders are absolutely strict. I am to let no one go across, no matter what his rank."

The chaplain considered a moment, but he did not move from where he stood beside the sergeant.

A minute passed and a chaplain of the Presbyterian faith came up. "Sergeant, I want to go across to those men. They are in a bad way."

"I know, sir. Sorry, sir. Strict orders that no one must be allowed to pass."

"Who are your orders from?"

"High authority, sir."

"Ah!" The padre looked at the sergeant....

"Sorry, Sergeant, but I have orders from a Higher Authority," and the Presbyterian minister rushed across the bullet-swept area. He fell dead before he reached his objective.

"I, too, have orders from a Higher Authority," said the Roman Catholic priest, and he dashed out into the roadway. He fell, dead, close by the body of his Protestant brother. They had not reached the wounded, but Heaven is witness that their death was the death of men.

Hand in hand with the chaplains at the front is the Y.M.C.A. It is doing a marvelous work among the troops. The Y.M.C.A. huts are scattered all over the fighting front. Here you will find the padre with his coat off engaged in the real "shirt-sleeve" religion of the trenches. Here there are all possible comforts, even little luxuries for the boys. Here are concerts,—the best and best-known artists come out and give their services to cheer up Tommy. Here the padres will hold five or six services in an evening for the benefit of the five or six relays of men who can attend. Here are checker-boards, chess sets, cards, games of all sorts. Here is a miniature departmental store where footballs, mouth organs, pins, needles, buttons, cotton, everything can be bought.

"What's the place wid the red triangle?" asked the Irish soldier, lately joined up and only out, from a Scotch-Canadian who stood near by.

"Yon? D'ye mean to say ye dinna know the meaning o' thon? Why, mon, yon's the place whaur ye get a packet o' fags, a bar o' chocolate, a soft drink and salvation for twenty-five cents."

Yes; we get all that in the Y.M.C.A. huts where the padre toils and the layman sweats day and night for the well-being of the soldier men. In some of the huts it is actually possible to get a bath. It is always possible to get dry. 'Twas Black Jack Vowel, good friend Jack, who wrote over to tell us that there was no hut at one time near his front.

"Bad luck here, this time in. No Y.M.C.A. hut near. I was coming out last night for a turn in billets when I fell into a shell hole. It was pretty near full of water, so I got soaked to the neck, and I hit against a couple of dead Boches in it, too. Not nice. Reached the billet dripping wet. Have got a couple of sugar boxes, one at my head and one at my feet. Have coke brazier underneath. If I lie here about three hours and keep turning, I guess I'll be dry by then."

That's when no padre was handy to lead the way to a hut.

Can folk wonder why we love the padres, why we reverence the Y.M.C.A.? Can folk wonder why the men who used to look on such men as sissy-boys have changed their opinions? Can folk wonder that the religion which is Christian is making an impression on the soldier? Can folk deny the fact that this war will make better men?

Once again I mention Major the Reverend John Pringle. Best of pals, best of sports, best of sky-pilots! Many a time as we have been marching along we have met him. He would pick out a face from among the crowd, maybe a British Columbia man. "Hello! salmon-belly!" would good Major John peal out. Again, he would see a Nova Scotian: "Hello! fish-eater—hello, blue-nose!"

Then through us all would go a rush of good feeling and good heart. Through all of us would go a stream of courage and happiness and a desire to stand right with the man as he was.

"Hello! Sky-pilot!"

CHAPTER XI

VIVE LA FRANCE ET AL BELGE!

We had only been about ten weeks in France when we were moved out of the trenches and placed in Ypres in billets. Some of us were actually billeted in the city itself, and others of us had a domicil in the environs.

Ypres, or Wipers, as Tommy Atkins called it, was then considered a "hot" spot. The Germans say no one ever comes back from Ypres without a hole in him. Tommy says, when he curses, "Oh, go to ——; you can't last any longer than a snow ball in Ypres!"

At this time Ypres was not yet destroyed by the enemy. I have seen many cities of the world. I have seen the beauties of Westminster Abbey, the Law Courts; I have seen the tropical wonders of the West Indies; I have seen the marvels of the Canadian Rockies, but I have never seen greater beauty of architecture and form than in the city of Ypres. There was the Cloth Hall, La Salle des Draperies with its massive pillars, its delicate traceries, its Gothic windows and its air of age-long gray-toned serenity.

There was Ypres Cathedral! A place of silence that breathed of Heaven itself. There was its superb bell tower, and its peal of silver-tongued chimes. There were wonderful Old World houses, quaint steps and turns and alleys. It was a city of delight, a city that charmed and awed by its impressive grandeur.

Now the city was massed with refugees from the ravaged parts of Belgium. In peace times possibly the population would have numbered thirty-five to forty thousand, at this time it seemed that sixty thousand souls were crowded into the city limits. Every house, every *estaminet*, every barn, every stable was filled to its capacity with folk who had fled in despair before the cloven hoof of the advancing Hun.

Glance at the map on page 142 and judge of the condition of a city practically surrounded on all sides by the enemy. Three miles away to the left, three miles away to the right, and a matter of only ten miles away from the immediate front of the city. For months the Germans had shelled the town every day. Not with a continued violence, but with a continued, systematic irritation which played havoc with the strongest nerves. Not a day passed that two or three women, or half a dozen children or babies did not pay the toll to the war god's lust of blood.

But still the people remained in the city. There was no alternative. Conditions behind Ypres were just the same, and all the way back to Calais. Every town and every village, every hamlet and every farm had its quota of refugees. Here they stayed and waited grimly for the day of liberation.

One day I walked out from Ypres a few miles. I came to the village of Vlamentinge. I went into an *estaminet* and called for some refreshment. From among the crowd of soldiers gathered there a civilian Belgian made his way over to me. He was crippled or he would not have been in civilian clothes.

"Hello, old boy!" he said to me in perfect English. "How are you?"

I replied, but must have looked my astonishment at his knowledge of my language, for he went on to explain.

"I got over from the States just the week war broke out. I worked in North Dakota, and had saved up and planned to come over and marry my sweetheart, who waited in Brussels for me. I have not seen her. She must be lost in the passing of the enemy. I have gathered a very little money, enough to start on the small farm which is my inheritance. Come and see it—come and have dinner with me."

I accepted his invitation, and we walked over together. The Belgian spoke all the way of his fine property and good farm. All the while there was a twinkle in his eye, and at last I asked him what size was his great farm.

"Ten acres," said he, and laughed at my amazement at so small a holding.

We reached the house, which proved to be a three-roomed shack. In a little, dinner was served and we went in to sit down. Not only the owner and myself, but fifteen others sat down to a meal of weak soup and war bread. The other guests at the table were fourteen old women and one young girl. They sat in a steady brooding silence. I asked the Belgian if they understood English. They did not, and so I questioned him.

"Very big family this you've got," I remarked. I knew what they were, but just wanted to draw him out.

"Oh, they're not my family."

"Only visitors?" I queried.

"Darned good visitors," said he, "they've been here since the second week of August, 1914."

"Refugees—" I commented.

"Yes, refugees, not one with a home. Not one who has not lost her husband, her son or her grandson. Not one who has not lost every bit of small property, but her clothes as well. You think that I am doing something to help? Well, that is not much. I'm lucky with the few I have. There's my old neighbor over yonder on the hill. He owns five acres and has a two-roomed shack and he keeps eleven."

"And how long do you expect them to stay?"

"Why, laddie," said he. "Stay—how should I know? I was talking to an officer the other day and he told me he believed the first ten years of this war would be the worst. They are free and welcome to stay all that time, and longer if need be. They are my people. They are Belgians. We have not much. My savings are going rapidly, but we have set a few potatoes"—he waved his hand over to where four of the old women were hoeing the ground. "We get bread and a little soup; we have enough to wear for now. We shall manage."

That is only one instance in my own personal experience. Every place was the same. The people who could, sheltered those that had lost all. It was a case of share and share alike. If one man had a crust and his neighbor none, why then each had half a crust without questions.

It is for Belgium. It is to-day, in the midst of war and pillage and outrage, that man is learning the brotherhood of man. In peace times no man would have imagined the possibility of sharing his home and income, no matter how great it might have been, with fifteen other persons. The fifteen unfortunates would have been left to the tender mercies of a precarious and grudging charity. To-day, charity is dead in its old accepted sense of doling out a few pence to the needy; to-day, charity is imbued with the spirit of Him who, to the few said, "I was hungered and you gave me meat."

To-day, it is not necessary to go to Ypres, to Namur, to Liége, to Verdun, or to any of the bombarded cities of Belgium and France to see the ruin that has been wrought by war among the people. It is the populace who suffer, even in greater degree than do the fighting men. They must give way in every instance before the irresistible barrier of martial law. It is the old men, the women, the children, the babies and the physically imperfect who must bear the brunt of dreadfulness.

Go to any of the cities of France, a hundred or more miles from the firing line. Go to Rouen, to Paris, to the smaller inland towns, to St. Omer, to Aubreville, and there is war.

The streets and boulevards, which a few years since were gay with a laughing crowd of joyous-hearted men and women, youths and maidens, to-day are gloomy, with the shadow of sorrow and death on them. On a conservative estimate it will be found that in all the towns and cities of France, one in three women will be dressed in black.

The French woman carries through life the tradition of the veil. She is christened, and over her baby face there lies a white veil. She is confirmed, and a veil drapes her childish head. She is married, and a trailing lace veil half conceals her happy smiles. She mourns, and a heavy veil of black crape covers her from head to foot.

We of the Canadians learned to know the wonderful emotion of the French. As we marched along the streets we would see a Frenchwoman approaching us. She recognized the strange uniform of an Ally and her eyes would sparkle, and perchance she'd greet us with a fluttering handkerchief. The shadow of a smile would cross her face; she was glad to see us; she wanted to welcome us. And then she would remember, remember that she had lost her man—her husband, her son, her sweetheart. He had been just as we, strong and virile. He had gone forth to a victory that now he was never to see on earth. His had been the supreme sacrifice. She would pass us, and the tears would come to her eyes, and we'd salute those tears—for France.

Over the top

And the men, what of them? There are no men. You will see old men, shaken and weak; possibly they have experienced the German as he was in 1870, and they know. You will see boys, eager strong boys, who impatiently await the call to arms. You will see young men who now look old. You will see them blind, and led about by a younger brother or sister. You will see the permanently crippled and those that wait for death, a slow and lingering death from the Hun's poisonous gases.

With the best of luck

It is no uncommon sight to see the peasantry of France and Belgium, the old and young women, the children and the very old men, working in their fields and on their tiny farms, less than a mile from the trenches. It is their home. It is France or it is Belgium, and love of country and that which is theirs is stronger than fear of death. Some one of them may be blown to pieces as he works; it makes no difference. They do not leave as long as it is possible to remain, or as long as the Allied armies will permit them to stay.

Their houses may be leveled, they may only find shelter in a half ruined cellar. Often they may go hungry, but always there is a grim determination to stick to their own, to till the ground which has kept them, which has kept their parents and great-grandparents, and which they mean shall keep their children when victory, which they know is inevitable, is complete.

They have a wonderful faith.

The casualties of the French army have never been made public. We do not know them. It may be that they will never be told to a curious world. France may have had her body crushed almost beyond endurance, but the unspeakable Hun—the barbarian, the crusher of hope and love and ideals—has not even made a dent on the wonderful spirit of France.

France is superb. In the parlance of the man in the street, we all "take off our hats" to this valiant country.

I could tell of the most horrible things possible for human mind to conceive. I have seen things that, put in type, would sicken the reader. I do not want to tell of these things here, evidence of them can be had from any official document or blue-book. And yet, in justice to Belgium, I must tell some of the least dreadful of the things I have seen and only those that have come to me through personal experience. I do not tell from hearsay, and I tell the truth without exaggeration.

In common with thousands of other Canadian and Imperial soldiers I saw the evacuation and destruction of Ypres. On the morning of April 21, 1915, we marched along the Ypres-Menin road, which road was the key to Calais, to Paris, to London and to New York. We marched along in the early hours of the morning, just after dawn. To our left passed a continuous stream of refugees. We looked toward them as we went by. We saluted as they passed, but many of us had dimmed vision.

We had heard of German atrocities. We had seen an isolated case or two as we marched from town to town and village to village. We had not paid a great deal of attention to them, as we had considered such things the work of some drunken German soldier who had run riot and defied the orders of the officers. Though we had certainly seen one or more cases that had impressed us very deeply. The case I cited earlier in this book never left my thoughts. But here on the king's highway, we saw

German atrocities on exhibition for the first time. I say exhibition, and public exhibition, because it was the first time we had seen atrocities in bulk—in numbers—in hundreds.

Ypres had been destroyed in seven hours, after a continuous bombardment from one thousand German guns. It was a city of the dead. The military authorities of the Allies told the civilians they must leave. They had to go, there was no alternative. The liberation they had hoped for was in sight, but their road to it was of a roughness unspeakable.

There was the grandfather in that procession, and the grandmother,—sometimes she was a crippled old body who could not walk. Sometimes she was wheeled in a barrow surrounded by a few bundles of household treasure. Sometimes a British wagon would pass piled high with old women and sick, to whom the soldiers were giving a lift on their way.

There was the mother in that procession. Sometimes she would have a bundle, sometimes she would have a basket with a few broken pieces of food. There was a young child, the baby hardly able to toddle and clinging to the mother's skirts. There was the young brother, the little fellow, whimpering a little perhaps at the noise and confusion and terror which his tiny brain could not grasp. There was the baby, the baby which used to be plump and smiling and round and pinky white, now held convulsively by the mother to her breast, its little form thin and worn because of lack of nourishment.

There was no means of feeding these thousands of helpless ones. Their only means of sustenance was from the charity of the British and French soldiers, who shared rations with them.

And there was sister, the daughter—sister—sister. At sight of these young girls—from thirteen up to twenty and over—we learned, if we had not learned before, that this is a war in which every decent man must fight. Some Americans and Canadians may not want to go overseas; they may be opposed to fighting; they may think they are not needed. Let them once see what we saw that April morning and nothing in the world could keep them at home.

They dragged along with heads low, and eyes seeking the ground in a shame not of their own making. I am conservative when I say that one in four of the hundreds of young girls who walked along in that sad crowd had a baby, or was about to have one.

And that was not the only horror of their situation. Many of them had one or the other arm off at the elbow. They had not only been ruined, but mutilated by their barbarous enemies.

That evening we camped just outside the city of Ypres. We rested all night, and the next day we went into action. During the afternoon of April twenty-second the Germans, for the first time in the history of warfare, used poisonous gas. And they used it against us as we lay there ready to protect the Ypres salient.

CHAPTER XII

CANADIANS—THAT'S ALL

Less than three months before this we were raw recruits. We were considered greenhorns and absolutely undisciplined. We had had little of trench experience. At Neuve Chapelle we had "stood by." At Hill 60 we had watched the fun. But our discipline, our real mettle, had not yet been put to the test.

That evening of the twenty-second of April when we marched out from Ypres, little did any of us realize that within the next twenty-four hours more than one-half of our total effectives were to be no more.

I feel sure that our commanders must have been nervous. They must have wondered and asked themselves, "Will the boys stand it?" "How will they come out of the test?"

We were about to be thrown into the fiercest and bitterest battle of the war. There were no other troops within several days' march of us. There was no one to back us up. There was no one else, should we fail, to take our place. "Canadians! It's up to you!"

I could tell of several stirring things that happened to other battalions during that night, but I am only telling of what I saw myself, and it will suffice to write of one most stirring thing which befell the Third.

As we crossed the Yser Canal we marched in a dogged and resolute silence. No man can tell what were the thoughts of his comrade. We have no bands, nor bugles, nor music when marching into action. We dare not even smoke. In dark and quiet we pass steadily ahead. There is only the continued muffled tramp—tramp—of hundreds of feet encased in heavy boots.

To the far right of us and to the far left shells were falling, bursting and brilliantly lighting up the heavens for a lurid moment. In our immediate sector there were no shells. It was all the more dark and all the more silent, for the noise and uproar and blazing flame to right and left.

We were on rising ground now. Up and up steadily we went. We reached the top of the grade, when suddenly from out of the pit of darkness ahead of us there came a high explosive shell. It dropped in the middle of our battalion. It struck where the machine gun section was placed, and annihilated them almost to a man.

Then it was that our mettle stood the test. Then it was that we proved the words Canadian and Man synonymous. Not one of us wavered; not one of us swerved to right or left, to front or back. We kept on. There was hardly one who lost in step. The commanders whispered in the darkness, "Close up the ranks." The men behind those who had fallen jumped across the bodies of their comrades lying prone, and joined in immediately behind those in the forward rows.

The dead and wounded lay stretched where they had fallen. Coming behind us were the stretcher-bearers and the hospital corps. We knew our comrades would have attention. This was a grim business. We pressed on.

There was a supreme test of discipline. It was our weighing time in the balance of the world war, and we proved ourselves not wanting. We were Canadians—that's all.

That afternoon the gas came over on us. The Germans put gas across on us because they hated us most. It is a compliment to be hated by the Germans. Extreme hatred from a German in the field shows that the hated are the most effective. They hated the French most at first, they hated the Imperial British, they hated us; they have hated the English again; soon, when the

United States comes to her full effectiveness, she will take her place in the front rank of the hated.

We Canadians were a puzzle to them. When we went into the trenches at first, the enemy would call across the line to us, "What have you come over here to fight us for? What business is it of yours? Why did you not stay back home in Canada and attend to your own affairs, and not butt into something that does not concern you? If you had stayed at home in your own country, WHEN WE CAME OVER AND TOOK CANADA, we would have treated you all right. Now that you have interfered, we are going to get you some day and get you right."

Yes; when they came over and took Canada. That was the very reason we were fighting. We wanted to keep our own part of the empire for ourselves. It is ours absolutely, and we had no intention that Germany should own it. We knew exactly what the Hohenzollern planned to do. If France were subdued, if England were beaten on her own ground, then Canada would be a prize of war. We preferred to fight overseas, in a country which already had been devastated, rather than carry ruin and devastation into our own land, where alone we would not have had the slightest chance in the world for beating Germany.

In the front lines of the Ypres salient was the Third Brigade, made up of Canadian Highlanders, whom the Germans, since that night have nicknamed "The Ladies from Hell." In this brigade were men from parts of Nova Scotia, Montreal, from Hamilton, Toronto, Winnipeg and Vancouver.

To the left of these lay the Second Brigade of Infantry. These were men for the most part from the West. There was the Fifth, commonly known as the "Disappointed Fifth," from Regina, Moose Jaw and Saskatoon. There was the Eighth, nicknamed by the Germans "The Little Black Devils from Winnipeg." The Tenth, the famous "Fighting Tenth," with boys from Southern Alberta, mainly Medicine Hat and Calgary and Lethbridge. And there was the Seventh of British Columbia.

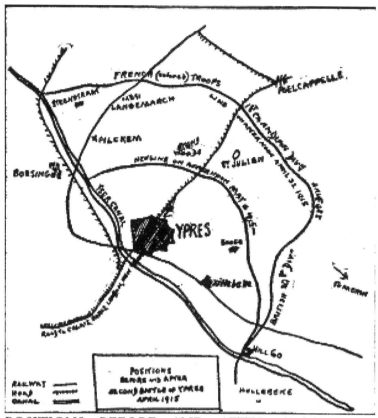

POSITIONS BEFORE AND AFTER SECOND
BATTLE OF YPRES APRIL 1915

It was the Second Brigade which the First was
supporting. To the left of the Eighth Battalion, which
was the extreme Canadian left wing, there were Zouaves
and Turcos. These were black French Colonials. To these
unfortunates, probably the Canadians owe their near
disaster.

In the far distance we saw a cloud rise as though from the earth. It was a greeny-red color, and increased in volume as it rolled forward. It was like a mist rising, and yet it hugged the ground, rose five or six feet, and penetrated to every crevice and dip in the ground.

We could not tell what it was. Suddenly from out the mist we men in reserves saw movement. Coming toward us, running as though Hell as it really was had been let loose behind them, were the black troops from Northern Africa. Poor devils, I do not blame them. It was enough to make any man run. They were simple-minded fellows. They were there to fight for France, but their minds could not grasp the significance of the enemy against whom they were pitted. The gas rolled on and they fled. Their officers vainly tried to stem the flying tide of them. Their heels barely seemed to touch the ground. As they ran they covered their faces, noses and eyes with their hands, and through blackened lips, sometimes cracked and bleeding, they gasped, "Allemands! Allemands!"

Some of our own French-speaking officers stopped the few running men they could make hear, and begged of them to reform their lines and go back to the attack. But they were maddened as only a simple race can be frenzied by fear, and paid no heed.

It is in times like this, in moments of dire emergency, that the officer of true worth stands out, the real leader of men. There were a dozen incidents to prove this in the next few hurried, desperate moments. None can be more soul-stirring than the quick thought, quick action and foresight displayed by our own captain. He did not know what this smoke rushing toward our lines could be. He had no idea more definite than any of us in the ranks. But he had that quick brain that acts automatically in an emergency and thinks afterward.

"Wet your handkerchiefs in your water-bottles, boys!" he ordered.

We all obeyed promptly.

"Put the handkerchiefs over your faces—and shoot like the devil!" he panted.

We did this, and as the gas got closer, the handkerchiefs served as a sort of temporary respirator and saved many of us from a frightful death. We in the reserves suffered least. Yet some of us died by that infernal product. A man dies by gas in horrible torment. He turns perfectly black, those men at any rate whom I saw at that time. Black as black leather, eyes, even lips, teeth, nails. He foams at the mouth as a dog in

hydrophobia; he lingers five or six minutes and then—
goes West.

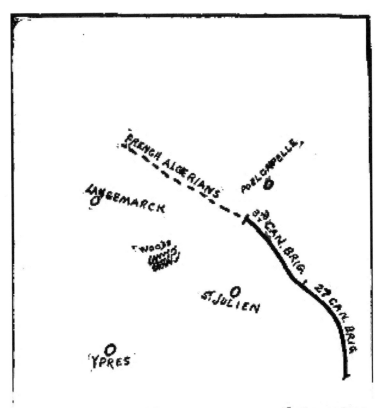

Position on April 22nd '15--BEFORE FIRST GAS
ATTACK

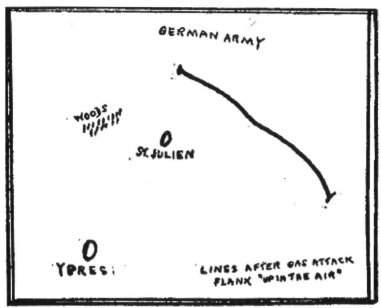

LINES AFTER GAS ATTACK FLANK "UP IN THE AIR"

Marvelous is the only word to describe the endurance, the valor of the Ladies from Hell. They withstood the gas, and they withstood wave after wave of attacking German hordes. And yet even their wonderful work was overtopped by that of the Eighth, which, being exposed on the left by the black troops who had fled, had to bear the brunt of a fight which almost surrounded them.

It was wonderful. I shall never forget it. There were twelve thousand Canadian troops. In the German official reports after the battle, they stated that they had used one hundred and twenty thousand men against us, and one thousand guns. We had not one gun. Those that we had were captured when the African blacks had left. It was our strength against theirs—no, it was white man's spirit against barbarian brutality.

For six days and nights that terrible death struggle continued. Every man was engaged: cooks, doctors, stretcher-bearers, chaplains, every one of us held a rifle. The wounded who had to take their chance of living because there was no way to convey them back to shelter—some of them would sit up, if they possibly could, to load and load again rifles which they lifted from dead comrades. They would hand us these as our rifles got too hot to hold. And still the German attacks persisted. Still they came on. And still we did not budge an inch from our position as it was when the gas first came over. They did not gain a yard, though when the British reserves at last reached us, there were only two thousand of us left standing on our feet; two thousand of us who were whole from out the twelve thousand that had started in to repel the attack.

The two thousand of us were still in the old position. Still we held in our safe-keeping the key of the road to Calais, to Paris, to London and farther. The key to world power which the Hohenzollern coveted.

Behind Ypres to-day there lie four thousand five hundred of the flower of the Canadian contingent. Four thousand five hundred young men who made the extreme sacrifice for King, for Flag, for Country, for Right. They lie in their narrow beds of earth, and over them wave the shading leaves of maple trees. For thoughtful citizens sent over and had planted "Canada's little maple grove"—a monument in a strange country to the men who fought and died and were not defeated.

On the night of April twenty-second, General Alderson and his officers saw that the situation was desperate. They thought to save their men. The general sent up the command: "Retire!"

The word first reached the Little Black Devils. The men heard it, the officers heard it, and they looked over the flattened parapet of their trench. They saw the oncoming hordes of brutes in a hellish-looking garb, and they sent back the answer: "Retire be damned!"

The general, the officers, rested content. With a spirit such as these men showed even against desperate odds, nothing but victory could result.

The gas and the attacking waves of men poured on. We were not frightened. No; none of us showed fear. Warfare such as this does not scare men with red blood in their veins. The Germans judge others by themselves. A German can be scared, a German can be bluffed. They thought that we were of the same mettle, or lesser. At the Somme we put over on the enemy the only new thing that we have been able to spring during the whole three years—the tanks. Were they scared? They were terrified! They dropped rifles, bayonets, knapsacks, everything— and ran. Had not our tanks stuck in the awful mud of France, or had they a trifle more speed, I believe it might have been possible for us to have reached Berlin by this time.

It was because we could not be frightened that General French, then Commander-in-Chief of the British Expeditionary Force, cabled across the world on the morning of the twenty-third of April, "The Canadians undoubtedly saved the situation."

No word of definite praise, no eulogy, no encomiums. Just six words—"The Canadians undoubtedly saved the situation."

The night of April twenty-second was probably the most momentous time of the six days and nights of fighting. Then the Germans concentrated on the Yser Canal, over which there was but one bridge, a murderous barrage fire which would have effectively hindered the bringing up of reinforcements or guns, even had we had any in reserve.

During the early stages of the battle, the enemy had succeeded to considerable degree in turning the Canadian left wing. There was a large open gap at this point, where the French Colonial troops had stood until the gas came over. Toward this sector the Germans rushed rank after rank of infantry, backed by guns and heavy artillery. To the far distant left were our British comrades. They were completely blocked by the German advance. They were like rats in a trap and could not move.

At the start of the battle, the Canadian lines ran from the village of Langemarcke over to St. Julien, a distance of approximately three to four miles. From St. Julien to the sector where the Imperial British had joined the Turcos was a distance of probably two miles.

These two miles had to be covered and covered quickly. We had to save the British extreme right wing, and we had to close the gap. There was no question about it. It was our job. On the night of April twenty-second we commenced to put this into effect. We were still holding our original position with the handful of men who were in reserves, all of whom had been included in the original grand total of twelve thousand. We had to spread out across the gap of two miles and link up the British right wing.

Doing this was no easy task. Our company was out first and we were told to get into field skirmishing order. We lined up in the pitchy darkness at five paces apart, but no sooner had we reached this than a whispered order passed from man to man: "Another pace, lads, just another pace."

This order came again and yet again. Before we were through and ready for the command to advance, we were at least twice five paces each man from his nearest comrade.

Then it was that our captain told us bluntly that we were obviously outnumbered by the Germans, ten to one. Then he told us that practically speaking, we had scarcely the ghost of a chance, but that a bluff might succeed. He told us to "swing the lid over them." This we did by yelling, hooting, shouting, clamoring, until it seemed, and the enemy believed, that we were ten to their one.

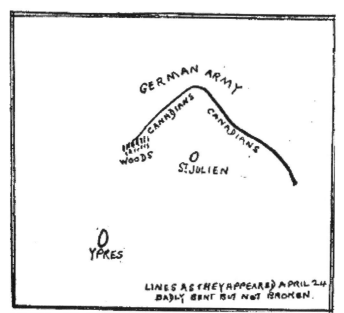

LINES AS THEY APPEARED, APRIL 24 BADLY BENT BUT NOT BROKEN

The ruse succeeded. At daybreak when we rested we found that we had driven the enemy back almost to his original position. All night long we had been fighting with our backs to our comrades who were in the front trenches. The enemy had got behind us and we had had to face about in what served for trenches. By dawn we had him back again in his original position, and we were facing in the old direction. By dawn we had almost, though not quite, forced a junction with the British right.

The night of April twenty-second is one that I can never forget. It was frightful, yes. Yet there was a grandeur in the appalling intensity of living, in the appalling intensity of death as it surrounded us.

The German shells rose and burst behind us. They made the Yser Canal a stream of molten glory. Shells fell in the city, and split the darkness of the heavens in the early night hours. Later the moon rose in a splendor of spring-time. Straight behind the tower of the great cathedral it rose and shone down on a bloody earth.

Suddenly the grand old Cloth Hall burst into flames. The spikes of fire rose and fell and rose again. Showers of sparks went upward. A pall of smoke would form and cloud the moon, waver, break and pass. There was the mutter and rumble and roar of great guns. There was the groan of wounded and the gasp of dying.

It was glorious. It was terrible. It was inspiring. Through an inferno of destruction and death, of murder and horror, we lived because we must.

Early in the night the Fighting Tenth and the Sixteenth charged the wood of St. Julien. Through the undergrowth they hacked and hewed and fought and bled and died. But, outnumbered as they were, they got the position and captured the battery of 4.7 guns that had been lost earlier in the day.

This night the Germans caught and crucified three of our Canadian sergeants. I did not see them crucify the men, although I saw one of the dead bodies after. I saw the marks of bayonets through the palms of the hands and the feet, where by bayonet points this man had been spitted to a barn door. I was told that one of the sergeants was still alive when taken down, and before he died he gasped out to his saviors that when the Germans were raising him to be crucified, they muttered savagely in perfect English, "If we did not frighten you before, this time we will."

I know a sergeant of Edmonton, Alberta, who has in his possession to-day the actual photographs of the crucified men taken before the dead bodies were removed from the barnside.

Again I maintain that war frightfulness of this kind does not frighten real men. The news of the crucified men soon reached all of the ranks. It increased our hatred. It doubled our bitterness. It made us all the more eager to advance—to fight—to "get." We had to avenge our comrades. Vengeance is not yet complete.

In the winter of 1914-1915 the Germans knew war. They had studied the game and not a move was unfamiliar to them. We were worse than novices. Even our generals could not in their knowledge compare with the expertness of those who carried out the enemy action according to a schedule probably laid down years before.

We knew that on the day following the terrible night of April twenty-second we must continue the advance, that we dare not rest, that we must complete the junction with the right wing of the British troops. And the enemy knew it, too.

We expected that the Germans would be entrenched possibly one hundred or even two hundred yards from our own position, but not so. His nearest entrenchment was easily a mile to a mile and a half across the open land from us.

The reason for this distance was simple enough. We had succeeded in our bluff that we had many hundreds more of men than in reality was the case. The enemy calculated that had we this considerable number of troops we would capture his trenches, were he to take a position close in, with one short and mad rush. He further calculated that had we even a million men, he would have the best of us if we attempted to cross the long, open flat land in the face of his thousands of machine guns.

April twenty-third was one of the blackest days in the annals of Canadian history in this war, and again it was one of the most glorious. That day we were given the task of retaking the greater part of the trenches which the Turco troops had lost the day preceding.

We lay, my own battalion, easily a mile and a half from the German trench which was to be our objective. About six o'clock in the morning we set out very cautiously, with Major Kirkpatrick in command. C and D Companies were leading, with a platoon or two of B Company following, comprising in all about seven hundred and fifty men. At first we thought the advance would be comparatively easy, but when we entered the village of St. Julien, the German coal boxes were falling all around us. So far our casualties were light.

To the left of the village we formed in field skirmishing order—about five paces apart—but before the formation of five successive lines or waves was completed, each man was easily eight paces away from his nearest mate instead of five. We were told that our objective was an enemy trench system about four hundred yards in length.

It is impossible to convey in words the feeling of a man in such a situation as this. Apparently none of us actually realized the significance of what we were about to undertake. Probably it was because we were no longer in the trenches, and because we had been out and in the open all the night before.

We stood there waiting. Overhead there was the continuous "Crack, crack, crack!" of enemy machine gun and other bullets. It was evident that we had already traversed a mile of our way, and that only half a mile lay ahead of us. The enemy bullets were flying high. I heard no command; I do not think any command was given in words, but of a sudden we heard a "Click!" to the left. No one even glanced in the direction. Every man fixed his bayonet. The man on the extreme left had fixed his, the "Click" had warned his comrades eight paces away, and the ominous sound, ominous for Hans and Fritz, "Click, click, click!" ran along the lines.

The advance had started. In front were our officers, every one of them from junior to senior, well ahead of their men. A wave of the hand, a quarter right turn, one long blast of the whistle and we were off. We made mad rushes of fifty or sixty yards at a time, then down we would go. No place to seek cover, only to hug Mother Earth.

Our lads were falling pretty fast; our officers even faster. To my left Slim Johnstone got his; ahead of me I saw Billy King go down. I heard some one yell out that Lieutenant Smith had dropped. In the next platoon Lieutenant Kirkpatrick fell dead. A gallant lad, this; he fell leading his men and with a word of cheer on his lips.

We were about two hundred yards from the enemy's trench and my estimation is that easily one-third of our fighting men were gone. Easily eighty per cent. of our officers were out of the immediate game. Right in front of our eyes our captain—Captain Straight—fell. As he went down he blew two short blasts on his whistle, which was the signal to hug the earth once more. And we dropped.

The officers and men who had been hit had begun their weary crawl back to the dressing station; that is, all of them who were able to make the effort. We saw that Captain Straight made no attempt to move. Some of us crept up to his side.

"Hit in the upper leg," he whispered in reply to the queries.

"Go back, sir, go back!" we urged, but Captain Straight was obdurate. He had made up his mind that he was going to see the thing through, and stick to it he would no matter what the cost to himself. He realized that only by some super-human effort would we now be able to take the enemy trench. The machine gun fire was hellish. The infantry fire was blinding. A bullet would flash through the sleeve of a tunic, rip off the brim of a cap, bang against a water-bottle, bury itself in the mass of a knapsack. It seemed as though no one could live in such a hail of lead. But no one had fallen down on the task of the day. Each battalion was advancing, with slowness and awful pain, but all were advancing.

Captain Straight knew how we were placed for effectives, both in officers and men. He knew how we adored him. He lay a few minutes to get his breath, then attempted to stand, but could not, as one leg was completely out of commission. He dragged himself along with his hands, catching hold of the tufts of grass or digging his fingers into the soft earth. He made thirty or forty yards in this way, then one long blast of his whistle and we rushed ahead, to fall flat on a level with him as he sounded the two-blast command. Probably ten times he dragged himself forward, and ten times we rushed and dropped in that awful charge. The captain gritted his teeth, for his pain must have been horrible. He waved his arm as he lay and waited ahead of us—"Come on, lads—come on!" And we came.

I don't know what other men may have felt in that last advance. For myself, the thought flashed across my mind—"What's the use? It is certain death to stay here longer; why not lie down, wait till the worst is over and be able to fight again—it is useless, hopeless—it is suicide to attempt such a task." Then just ahead of us I saw Captain Straight crawling slowly but surely, and through the "Zing!" of bullets I heard his voice, fainter but still earnest and full of courage, cry out: "Come on, lads—come on!"

He was one of the first to roll over into that improvised German trench.

No, we could not have failed; we could not have stopped. As one of our young boys said afterward: "Fellows, I'd have followed him to Hell and then some!"

It was Hell all right, but no matter; we had gone through it, and got what we had come for—the German trench.

Out of the seven hundred and fifty of us who advanced, a little over two hundred and fifty gained the German trench; and of that number twenty-five or more fell dead as soon as they reached the enemy, and got that revenge for which they had come.

I doubt if there will again be a battle fought in this war where the feeling of the men will be as bitter as at St. Julien. Men were found dead with their bayonets through the body of some Hun, men who had been shot themselves thirty yards down the field of advance. Their bodies were dead, as we understand death, but the God-given spirit was alive, and that spirit carried the earthbound flesh forward to do its work, to avenge comrades murdered and womanhood outraged. It was marvelous—it may have been a miracle. It was done, and for all time has proved to the boys who fought out there the power of the spirit over the flesh.

We had seen atrocities on the Belgians the day before. We had seen young girls who were mutilated and horribly maltreated. We had been gassed, we had seen our comrades die in an awful horror. We had had our sergeants crucified, and we were outnumbered ten to one. After all this, and after all the Hell through which we had passed from six that morning until after two, when we reached the enemy trench and presented the bright ends of our bayonets, Mr. Fritz went down on his knees and cried, "*Kamerad! Kamerad!*"

What did we do? We did exactly what you would have done under like circumstances. "*Kamerad!*"—Bah!

There is no doubt that the German soldier is a good soldier as far as he goes. He is good in a charge and if he had not done the despicable things—the dreadful outrages which he has done—he could be admired as a fighting machine. But there is one department where we of the Allies have him licked to a frazzle. Talk to any man who has been out there and he will say the same. The German soldier can not hold in a hand-to-hand fight. He can't face the cold steel. The second he glimpses the glint of a bayonet he is whimpering and asking for mercy.

The German bayonet is a fiendish weapon. It is well its owner can not use it. For myself I do not know of one case where a comrade has been wounded by enemy steel. His bayonet is longer than ours, and from the tip for a few inches is a saw edge. This facilitates entrance into the body, but on turning to take it out it tears and rends savagely.

It is impossible to describe the work of every battalion in a battle. In a charge, a concerted charge, such as we went through on April twenty-third, there was not one battalion that did better than another. There was not one officer who did better than another, there was not one man who outdistanced his fellow in valor. We all fought like the devil. It is only possible to convey the doings of the whole by telling the achievements of the few.

Boys of the Fourth Western Ontario Battalion, commanded by Colonel Birchall of St. Catharines, who came through this business, have told me that their colonel lined them up and made a short speech to them. He took them into his confidence. He told them that the whole battalion should advance together; that he did not think it good policy to leave any part in reserve. He said: "I am going to lead you, boys; will you come?"

There was a sonorous "Aye, aye, sir!" along the ranks.

Colonel Birchall pulled his revolver from its holster, looked at it a moment and then threw it to the ground. Then he took his small riding switch and hung the loop over the first finger of his right hand.

"Ready, boys!" he cried, and twirling the little cane round and round, he strode ahead.

It was a terrible piece of work. On every side shells and bullets were falling. Men went down like ninepins at a fair. But always ahead was the colonel, always there was the short flash of his cane as it swished through the air.

Then he was hit, a bullet in the upper right arm. He did not stop; he did not drop the cane.

"On, boys, on!" And the men stumbled up and forward.

Seven times Colonel Birchall was a mark for enemy fire. Seven times fresh wounds gushed forth with his life's blood. He was staggering a little now, but never a falter; on and on he went, the little cane feebly waving.

Men say that at times the lines seemed to waver and almost to break; that the whole advancing force, small and scattered though it was, seemed to bend backward as cornstalks in wind, but always they saw the colonel ahead and recovered balance.

Colonel Birchall fell dead on the parapet of the German trench, but he got what he had come after. His men were with him. There were seven hundred and more dead and wounded in the battalion, but the trench was theirs and Fritz was again begging for mercy.

There are stories, wonderful stories of stirring things done by the several battalions, but it is not possible to give them in detail. Men made undying names in this battle, names which will go down through the ages as have the names of other British soldiers. There was

Brigadier-General Turner, who is now Major-General, of the Third Brigade. There was Lieutenant-Colonel, now Brigadier-General, Watson of the Second Battalion, who, together with Lieutenant-Colonel Rennie, now Brigadier-General, of the Third Battalion, reinforced the Third Infantry Brigade. These two were of the First Brigade. Then there came the Seventh Battalion, which is the British Columbia Regiment of the Second Brigade, and the Tenth Battalion, also of the Second.

Lieutenant-Colonel Boyle commanded the Fighting Tenth, and gave his life in the advance. The Sixteenth Battalion Canadian Scottish were under command of Lieutenant-Colonel Leckie, who has since become Brigadier-General. The Tenth had many losses. Major MacLaren, second in command, died in hospital shortly after being taken there, and Major Ormond was wounded. Major Guthrie is another man who carried the Tenth forward to more triumphs. Brigadier-General Mercer, Lieutenant-Colonel Morrison, Captain T.E. Powers are others, and Lieutenant-Colonel, since Brigadier-General, Lipsett, commanded the Ninetieth Winnipeg Rifles, whose men suffered severely from gas.

Major Norsworthy was killed while trying to bring up reinforcements. He endeavored to reach Major McCuiag, who had the great misfortune, after doing marvelous work and saving an almost desperate situation, to be taken prisoner by the enemy. Men of the Seventh Battalion were Colonel Hart-McHarg, Major Odlum and Lieutenant Mathewson. The Second Brigade was under command of Brigadier-General Currie, who now is the Commander-in-Chief of the Canadian Expeditionary Forces.

Lieutenant-Colonel, now Brigadier-General, Armstrong, commanded the Engineers, but crowning all of these names is that of our beloved Commander-in-Chief at the time, General Alderson.

Ten thousand names more could be added to this gallant roll of honor. At the beginning of the battle of Ypres our lines were a little over twelve thousand strong, and after six days and nights of fighting there remained two thousand of us standing. We had practically not budged an inch. The Germans had not broken our line, our one thin, straggling, far-stretched line. We remained the victors of Ypres.

Perhaps our greatest reward came when on April twenty-sixth the English troops reached us. We had been completely cut off by the enemy barrage from all communication with other sectors of the line. Still, through the wounded gone back, word of our stand had drifted out. The English boys fought and force-marched and fought again their terrible way through the barrage to our aid. And when they arrived, weary and worn and torn, cutting their bloody way to us, they cheered themselves hoarse; cheered as they marched along, cheered and gripped our hands as they got within touch with us. Yell after yell went upward, and stirring words woke the echoes. The boys of the Old Country paid their greatest tribute to us of the New as they cried:

"Canadians—Canadians—that's all!"

CHAPTER XIII

TEARS AND NO CHEERS

On May third we commenced our withdrawal to Bailleul, leaving our sector of the line in safe hands. We were billeted in this town for a rest.

We were a haggard bunch. Our faces were drawn in lines like old men, many were gray, some were white; our eyes were wild and glassy and we moved jerkily or started at the slightest of sharp sounds.

Reinforcements began to arrive. We needed them. There were C and D Companies without an officer between them. Major Kirkpatrick was wounded and a prisoner; Captain Straight wounded and taken; Captain Johnson wounded and imprisoned; Lieutenant Jarvis, son of Amelius Jarvis, the famous sporting figure of Toronto, lay dead, and our gallant old Major Pete Anderson, our sniping officer, was also captured, though he has now escaped from enemy hands.

In billets we had thought we were hard hit. We had not realized it to the full till the morning we were lined up, one brigade at a time, for review. We had had an issue of fresh clothing, we had had some long hours of sleep, we had had all that soap and water could do for us, but we were a sorry and sorrowful lot of men. We had the light of triumph in our eyes, but even that was dimmed at thought of the boys who were gone to the great review above.

Our beloved commander-in-chief came along the lines to review us. He looked at us with the brave eyes of a father sorrowing over a dead son. He walked with head high and step firm, but his voice shook with deep emotion, and he did not hide the tears which rose to his eyes as he spoke his famous words of commendation.

They are immortal words, words which express the regret of a true man for comrades whose sacrifice was supreme, words which express pride in deeds done and breathe of a determination to greater deeds, if possible, in a triumphant future.

Words Spoken to the First Canadian Division
(Brigade by Brigade and to Engineers and Artillery)
After the Twelve Days and Nights of Fighting April 22d
to May 4th, 1915
By
Lieutenant-General E.A.H. Alderson
Commanding First Canadian Division

"All units, all ranks of the First Canadian Division, I tell you truly, that my heart is so full I hardly know how to speak to you. It is full of two feelings, the first being sorrow for the loss of those comrades of ours who have gone, the second—pride in what the First Canadian Division has done.

"As regards our comrades who have lost their lives, and we will speak of them with our caps off [here the general took off his cap, and all did likewise], my faith in the Almighty is such that I am perfectly sure that, in fact, to die for their friends, no matter what their past lives have been, no matter what they have done that they ought not to have done (as all of us do), I repeat that I am perfectly sure the Almighty takes care of them and looks after them at once. Lads—we can not leave them better than like that. [Here the general put his cap on, and all did the same.]

"Now, I feel that we may, without any false pride, think a little of what the Division has done during the past few days. I would first of all tell you that I have never been so proud of anything in my life as I am of this armlet '1 Canada' on it that I wear on my right arm. I thank you and congratulate you from the bottom of my heart for the part each one of you has taken in giving me this feeling of pride.

"I think it is possible that you do not, all of you, quite realize that if we had retired on the evening of the twenty-second of April when our Allies fell back from the gas and left our flank quite open, the whole of the Seventeenth and Twenty-eighth Divisions would probably have been cut off, certainly they would not have got away a gun or a vehicle of any sort, and probably not more than half the infantry. This is what our commander-in-chief meant when he telegraphed as he did: 'The Canadians undoubtedly saved the situation.' My lads, if ever men had a right to be proud in this world, you have.

"I know my military history pretty well, and I can not think of an instance, especially when the cleverness and determination of the enemy is taken into account, in which troops were placed in such a difficult position; nor can I think of an instance in which so much depended on the standing fast of one division.

"You will remember the last time I spoke to you, just before you went into the trenches at Sailly, now over two months ago, I told you about my old regiment—the Royal West Kents—having gained a reputation for not budging from the trenches, no matter how they were attacked. I said then that I was quite sure that in a short time the army out here would be saying the same of you.

I little thought—we, none of us thought—how soon those words would come true. But now, to-day, not only the army out here, but all Canada, all England, and all the Empire, is saying it of you.

"The share each unit has taken in earning this reputation is no small one.

"I have three pages of congratulatory telegrams from His Majesty the King downward which I will read to you, with also a very nice letter from our army commander, Sir Horace Smith-Dorrien.

"Now, I doubt if any divisional commander, or any division ever had so many congratulatory telegrams and messages as these, and remember they are not merely polite and sentimental ones; they express just what the senders feel.

"There is one word I would say to you before I stop. You have made a reputation second to none gained in this war, but remember, no man can live on his reputation, he must keep on adding to it. That you will do so I feel just as sure as I did two months ago when I told you that I knew you would make a reputation when the opportunity came.

"I am now going to shake hands with your officers, and I do so wanting you to feel that I am shaking hands with each one of you, as I would actually do if the time permitted.

"No—we will not have any cheering now—we will keep that until you have added to your reputation, as I know you will."

And there was no cheering. We turned away—the few men of us left whole in those scattered ranks—our eyes tear-dimmed in memory of those comrades whose lives had gone out; but our hearts ready to answer the call wherever it might lead us.

The world to-day knows what the Canadian boys have done. We have more than added to our reputation.

Right after this terrible scrap at Ypres came Givenchy and Festubert, and then we held the line at Ploegsteert for a whole year, fighting fiercely at St. Eloi, and stopping them again at Sanctuary Wood.

In the summer of 1916 fourteen thousand of us went down before German cannon, but still they did not break our lines. This was known as the third battle of Ypres.

From Ypres we went to the Somme, and it was on the Somme that we met our Australian cousins who jokingly greeted us with the statement "We're here to finish what you started," and we fired back, "Too bad you hadn't finished what you started down in Gallipoli!"

It was not very long before both were engaged in that terrible battle of the Somme, where to Canadian arms fell the honor of taking the village of Courcellette. We plugged right on and soon we put the "Vim" into Vimy, and took Vimy Ridge. As I write we are marking time in front of Lens.

At Ypres we started our great casualty lists with ten thousand. To-day over one hundred twenty-five thousand Canadian boys have fallen, and there are over eighteen thousand who will never come back to tell their story.

If the generals of the British Army were proud of us in 1915, I wonder how they feel to-day?

CHAPTER XIV

"THE BEST O' LUCK—AND GIVE 'EM HELL!"

Imagine a bright crisp morning in late September. The sun rises high and the beams strike with comforting warmth even into the fire-trench where we gather in groups to catch its every glint.

We feel good on such a morning. We clean up a bit, for things are quiet—that is, fairly quiet. Only a few shells are flying, there is little or no rifle fire and nobody is getting killed, nobody is even getting plugged.

The whole long day passes quietly. We are almost content with our lot. We laugh a good deal, we joke, we play the eternal penny ante, and possibly the letters come.

Just before stand-to at sundown the quiet will be broken. The artillery behind our lines will open up with great activity. We notice that the big shells only are being used and we notice that they are concentrating entirely on the German front line, immediately ahead and to the right and left of where we have our position. We are more than a little interested. There is decidedly something in the wind. We wait, but nothing happens. We have stand-to and get our reliefs for guard.

Every man has his bayonet fixed for the night. We give it a little extra polish. It may be needed soon. There is no outward show of nervousness. No man speaks to his neighbor of his immediate thoughts. We begin to smoke a little more rapidly, perhaps. We might have had a cigarette an hour during the heavy shelling of the day. During the night we will increase to one every half-hour, every twenty minutes. We light a fag, take a few puffs and throw it away. That is the only evidence of nerves.

We are in a state of complete ignorance as to what the outcome of this shelling may be. We have seen it just as severe before and nothing but a skirmish result. Some of us have seen shelling of the same intensity and have gone over the top and into a terrible mélange. We are always kept in ignorance; no commands and no orders are given. Did we know for hours ahead that at such and such a time we would go over the top, our nerves could hardly stand the strain. The noise, the terrific noise of our artillery bombarding the German trenches is hard enough on our nerves; what it must be on the nerves of the enemy is beyond conception. We do not wonder that in these latter days they fall on their knees and yell "*Kamerad*!"

As a rule a charge takes place just before dawn, when the gray cold light of morning is struggling up from the

East. All night we are occupied according to our individual temperaments. Some are able to sleep even in such a racket. The great majority of us are writing letters. There are always a few last things to be said to the home-folks, a few small possessions we want to will in special ways. We hand our letters to an officer or to some special chum. If this is to be our last time over—if it is to be our last charge—the officer or chum will see to it, if he lives, or the stretcher-bearers or the chaplains, if he doesn't, that the small treasures go back home to the old folks.

Just before dawn there is a difference in the character of the shelling. The heavy shells are falling farther back on German reserves and lighter artillery is being used on the enemy front line. The position lies some three hundred yards from the enemy front.

The light shells sweep close overhead as they go by our trench. We have to hug the sides close; sometimes the vacuum is so great that it will carry off a cap; if we are not careful it may suck up a head or lift us completely off our feet.

This curtain of fire continues for hours; it varies in direction now and then, but never in intensity. There is a controlling force over this tremendous bombardment. To my mind the most important man on the battle-field is he who holds the ordering of the bombardment—the observation officer. He must know everything, see everything, but must never be seen. During a heavy bombardment he works in conjunction with another observation officer. They are hidden away in any old place; it may be a ruined chimney, it may be a tree which is still left standing, or it may be in some hastily built up haystack. He controls the entire artillery in action on his special front, and he holds the lives of thousands of men in the hollow of his hand. One tiniest miscalculation and hundreds of us pay the price.

He is cool, imperturbable, calculating, ready in any emergency, good-tempered, deliberate and yet with the power to act instantly. At times he has command over a magnificent number of invectives!

As the minutes pass and the day lightens we smoke a fag every five minutes, every three minutes. The trench is filled with the blue gray smoke of thousands of cigarettes, lighted, puffed once, thrown away. It soothes our nerves. It gives us something to do with our hands. It takes our mind off the impending clash.

If we make an attack in broad daylight, which is seldom done except under a special emergency, the only command to charge will be the click, click, click of bayonets going into place all along the line. But charges are mostly made at gray-dawn, when bayonets are already fixed. Suddenly, away down the line we catch sight of one of our men climbing over the parapet. Then trench ladders are fixed, and in a twinkling every man of us is over the top with: "The best o' luck—and give 'em hell!"

We crawl out over the open. We reach our own barbed wire entanglements. We creep through them, round them, and out to No Man's Land. We are in it now for good and all.

The enemy is now concentrating his fire on our reserves. He knows that we have not had sufficient men in the front line trench to be of great effect. He knows that we can not fit them in there. He knows that the moment we have cleared the top of the parapet hundreds of men have poured from the communication trenches into our places. He knows that for miles back men are massed as thick as they can stand in the reserve trenches. His object is to destroy our reserves and not the immediate trench in front of him.

We follow the same plan. For, as we advance in short sharp rushes, the observation officer, who never for a moment relaxes his hold on the situation, flashes back by telegraph or field telephone the command to the artillery lying miles away to raise their curtain of fire. They do so, and shells fall on the German reserves, while we press forward, teeth bared and cold steel gleaming grayly, to take the front lines. We leap the parapet of the German trench. We spot our man and bear down on him. We clean out the dugouts and haul away the cowering officers, and already we are straightening and strengthening the German trench.

Behind us come wave on wave of our reserves. The second will take the second trench of the enemy; the third, the third, and so on. Then we consolidate our position, and Fritz is a sad and sorry boy.

That is the way it should work, but in the early days of the war we used to find this very difficult. We of the front line would charge and take our trench. We would get there and not a German to be seen! He would be beating it down his communication trenches, or what was left of them, as hard as he could go. We were supposed to stay in the front trench of the enemy. Well, it was simply against human nature, against the human nature of the First Canadian boys at any rate. We may have been out there for months and not had a chance to see a German. And had been wishing and waiting for this very opportunity. We would see Fritz disappear round a traverse and we simply could not stand still and let him go, or let the other fellow get him. We were bound to go after him. This was really our traditional weakness. Often-times we went too far in our eagerness to capture the Hun, and were unable to hold all that we got.

In the early days, too, we charged in open formation. Certainly we lost, in the first instance, fewer men by that method, but when we reached the enemy trench, took it, and had established ourselves therein, we were rarely strong enough in numbers to repulse the almost certain counter-attacks that came a few minutes or even an hour or so later.

We have altered this method now. We attack, not in the close formation, shoulder to shoulder, of the German, but in a formation which is a variation of his. We attack in groups of twenty or thirty men, who are placed shoulder to shoulder. If a shell comes over one group, it is obliterated, to be sure, but suppose no shell comes; then several such groups will reach the enemy lines, and Hans has not got the ghost of a chance once we get to close quarters. He has not the glimmer of a chance in a counter-attack when we have sufficient men to hold on to what we have gained.

On the other hand a German charge on our lines is a pretty sight. They advance at a dog-trot. They come shoulder to shoulder, each man almost touching his neighbor. They are in perfect alignment to start, and they lift their feet practically in exact time one with the other. Unlike us, they shoot as they advance. We have a cartridge in our magazine, but we have the safety catch on. We dare not shoot as we advance because our officers are always ahead, always cheering the boys forward. The German officer is always behind. He drives his men.

They shoot from the hip, but in that way their fire is never very effective. As they advance it is practically impossible to miss them, no matter how bad a shot any of us might be. We get fifteen rounds per minute from our rifles and our orders are to shoot low and to full capacity.

In the attacks of the enemy which I have seen they certainly have been brave. One must give them their due. It takes courage to advance in face of rifle fire, machine gun fire and artillery shells, in this close formation. Wave after wave of them come across in their field gray-blue uniforms and they never cower. One wave will be mowed down and another will quicken the pace a trifle and take its place. One man will go down and another will step into the gap. They are like a vast animated machine.

In one attack which we repulsed I am conservative when I say that they were lying dead and wounded three and four deep and yet they attacked again and again without faltering, only to be driven back to defeat in the end.

This war is not over yet by a long shot, and I should like to offer some advice to the boys who are going over from this continent. Our officers know better than we. The generals and aides who have been working on the problem, on the strategy and tactics during the three years gone by, are more qualified to conduct the war than the private who has lately joined. If you are told to stay in a certain place, then stay there. If you are told to dig in, you are a bad soldier if you don't dig and dig quickly. You are only a nuisance as long as you question authority. It does not pay. The boys of the First Division learned by experience. Do as you're told. The heads are taking no undue risks. Your life is as valuable to them as it is to you. They won't let you lose it unnecessarily. Get ahead and obey.

There is no need to lose your individuality. The vast difference between us and the enemy soldier is that we can think for ourselves should occasion arise; we can act on our own responsibility or we can lead if the need be.

Remember, that every single man is of importance. Each one is a cog in the vast organization and one slip may disrupt the whole arrangement. Obey, but use your intelligence in your obedience. Don't act blindly. Consider the circumstances and as far as you can use your reason as you believe the general or the colonel has used his. You are bounded only by your own small sector. What you know of other salients is hearsay. The general knows the situation in its entirety.

Obedience, a cool head, a clean rifle and a sharp bayonet will carry you far.

©Famous Players—Lasky Corporation. Scene from the
Photo-Play SHERMAN WAS NOT ALWAYS RIGHT.

Behind the barrage

CHAPTER XV

OUT OF IT

Every man who goes into the active service of the present war knows that someday, somehow, somewhere, he is going to get plugged. We have expressions of our own as to wounds. If a chap loses a leg or an arm or both, he'll say, "I lost mine," but when there is a wound, no matter how serious, yet which does not entail the loss of a visible part of the body, we say, "I got mine."

So it was as time wore on, I "got mine" in the right shoulder and right lung. A German explosive bullet caught me while I was in a lying position. It was at Ypres; we all get it at Ypres.

The thing happened under peculiar circumstances. It was the second time in my army career that I volunteered for anything. The first time was the night I went on listening post; the second time I got plugged, and plugged for good.

We had repulsed the enemy several times. We were running short of ammunition and our position was enfiladed. It was absolutely necessary, if all of us were not to lose our lives, that some one should bring up ammunition.

The ammunition dump lay about a mile back of our line. An officer called for volunteers to creep back for a supply. It was broad daylight, but twenty-eight other lads and myself stepped forward willing to attempt the task.

The men who remained behind had a command to keep up a rapid fire over the enemy trenches which would lend us some cover. No matter how perfect this covering may be, it is never completely effective in silencing the enemy fire. Quite a number of bullets scattered about us as we clambered along the short communication trench, and up into the open. This was my first experience in running away from bullets, and I proved in the first five seconds of that journey that a man, no matter what his propensities for winning medals may be, can run much faster from bullets than he can toward them.

Among us were boys of several other companies, and on the way out three of the twenty-nine got hit. I did not know whom. We kept on, breathless and gasping, running as we were under the weight of full equipment and dodging bullets as we went. Shells were falling round us too, now. We were not happy.

At last we got to our destination and picked up the boxes. A box of ammunition weighs a hundred or more pounds, so we decided that three of us should carry two boxes. The boxes are fitted with handles on each end.

We started off running at top speed, then dropping flat on our stomachs to fetch our breath and rest our aching arms. The enemy was rapidly getting thicker. We rose and rushed forward another stretch. At three hundred yards from the trench, the greater number of our crowd had fallen. We dropped. Then our hearts stood still, for from our trench there came a silence we could feel.

We knew what it meant. There was no need for the enemy to increase the rapidity of his fire over us and over the boys in the trench to let us know what was up. Our ammunition had already given out, and we had to face the last few hundred yards without protection, meager though it had been throughout. We knew there was not a man in that trench who had a bullet left. We knew that as far as we were concerned, we were done. We metaphorically shook hands with ourselves and wished friend self a long good-by. We looked at the sun and said "Tra-la-la" to it, and we wondered in a flash of thought what the old world would be like without us. We wondered where we would "light up."

All this passed in a moment of time, and then we decided that it would be better if we paired up, two men taking one box of ammunition. This offered a smaller target for the busy enemy, and also made for increased speed in covering the remaining ground.

We sprang up once more and dodged and doubled as we leaped through the rain of bullets, machine gun and rifle. How we lived I don't know. I was sharing a box with a lad whom I heard the fellows call Bob. He was no more than a boy, but we were much of a size and ran light. We were the only two of the twenty-nine left on our feet. To-day I am one of five of that bunch left alive.

About fifty yards from the trench we dropped for a last rest before the final spurt which would decide the whole course of events in the next ten minutes. Would we reach that trench and turn in our box of ammunition, or would we "get ours" and would the boys so eagerly waiting for us be surrounded and captured? Or would many of them do what they had threatened? "If it comes to surrendering," several had said in my hearing, "I will run a bayonet into myself rather than be taken."

When a man is lying close to the ground there is not so very great a chance of his being hit by bullets. They pass overhead as a rule. It is when a man is kneeling or standing, or between the two positions that the great danger lies. The lad Bob and I were just in the act of rising when mine came along. I felt no more than a stinging blow in the right shoulder, a searing cut and a thud of pain as the bullet exploded in leaving my body. I fell on my face and blood gushed from my shoulder.

"Hit hard or soft?" queried my companion, as he threw himself down beside me.

"Don't know," I gasped.

"You're hit in the mouth," he said, as the blood poured from between my lips.

"No, by gum, you're hit in the back!"

I gasped, nearly choked, and spluttered out: "You're a liar; I'm not hit in the back." But there was a gash in the back where the exploding missile had torn away and carried out portions of my lung and bits of bone and flesh.

I closed my eyes. Then from a distance I heard Bob speak.

"I'm going to fix you," he said, and knelt beside me. He got into such a position that his own body shielded me from any of the enemy bullets. It was a marvelous piece of bravery; less has earned a Victoria Cross.

He turned me round so that my head was toward our reserves and my feet were toward the Germans. In almost all cases when a man is hit he falls forward with his face to the enemy. In all probability he will become unconscious. When he awakes he remembers that he fell forward. A blind instinct works within him and makes him strive to turn around. He knows danger lies ahead, but friend and safety are back of him.

Bob shifted me round. "Remember," he whispered, "that if you should faint, when you come to you are placed right. You are in the right direction—don't turn round."

A wonderful motto for a man to carry through life. Bob had no thought of future or fame. In keen solicitude for a fallen comrade he uttered words which mean more in these days of war and blood than do the words of poets.

"You're in the right direction—don't turn round!"

Then the lad got up to go on. He struggled to lift the box of ammunition.

I whispered to him hoarsely: "You're not going on—you will never get there. It is certain death."

"Good-by, old boy," was his answer. "You don't think because the rest of you have gone down that I am going to be a piker. Say 'Hello!' to Mother for me should you see her before I do."

I have never seen his mother. I do not know her. If she lives she has the memory of a son who, though a boy in years, was a soldier and a very gallant gentleman. Bob tried to reach the trench, but a rain of bullets got him and he fell dead only a little way from me.

I lay where I had fallen for some time. I don't know how long, but long enough to see our boys captured by the enemy. And in so dreadful a plight as I was I had to smile. Those men who had boasted they would kill themselves, surrendered with the rest. Life is very sweet. There is always a chance of living, and always a chance of escape no matter how brutal the system in German prison camps.

Every man in that trench surrendered honorably. Not a man had a bullet left. They were hopelessly outnumbered, and it is hard to die when there is youth and love and strength.

As evening wore on I feared that I too might be captured, and I commenced a weary struggle to crawl back across the field. It was while I was resting after such an effort that a wonderful moment came to me. I saw the Lord Jesus upon His cross, and the compassion upon His face was marvelous to see. He appeared to speak to me.

"I am dying," I muttered, and then thought, "Shall I pray?"

Of outward praying I had done none. I thought about it and wondered. To pray now—no, that was being a piker. I had not prayed openly before, now when I was nearing death it was no time for a hurried repentance and a stammered prayer. I watched the vision as it slowly faded, and a great comfort surrounded me. I was happy.

I crawled on and reached a shell hole. It must have been an hour later that a despatch rider came to me. His motorcycle had been shot from under him, and he was striving to reach his destination on foot. He spoke to me, and then placed me in a blanket, which he took from a dead soldier. In this he dragged me to the shelter of an old tumbledown house. It had been riddled with shot and shell, but the greater part of the outer walls were standing, and it was shelter.

I begged the despatch rider to give me his name. I begged him to take some small things of mine to keep as a token for what he had done for me. But he would have nothing. He hurried away with the intention of sending help to me, and as he went I begged his name once more. "Oh! Johnnie Canuck!" said he. And there it remains. I do not know the name of the man who dragged me to comparative safety at such terrible risk to himself.

Behind the old house where I lay there was a battery of British guns, 4.7's. After a while the enemy found the range, and their shells commenced bursting round me. God in Heaven! I died a hundred deaths in that old ruin. Once a shell hit what roof there was and a score of bricks came crashing about me. Not one touched. I seemed charmed. I could hear the shells screeching through the air a second before they burst near where I lay. Of bodily pain I had little. The discomfort was great; the thirst was appalling. I thought I should bleed to death before help reached me. But there was nothing to compare with the mental strain of waiting—waiting—waiting for a shell to burst. Where would it drop? Would the next get me?

I hoped and longed and waited, but help did not come. I never lost consciousness. Darkness came and dawn. Another day went by and the shelling went on as before. Another night, another dawn and then two

Highland stretcher-bearers came in. They raised me gently. The bleeding had stopped, but that journey on the stretcher was too much. I had been found and I let myself drift into the land of unknown things.

I woke before we reached a dugout dressing station. Here I was given a first-aid dressing and immediately after carried away to an old-fashioned village behind the lines. At this point there was a rough field hospital, an old barn probably. There were eighty or ninety wounded there when I arrived. Among the many French and British were some Germans. The very next stretcher to me was occupied by one of the enemy.

The Red Cross floated over the building, but that emblem of mercy made no difference to the Hun. The shells commenced to find range, and in a short time the roof was lifted off. A wounded man died close to me. I can only remember the purr of a motor as an ambulance rushed up. Then I saw four stretcher-bearers; two grabbed the German, and two caught hold of me. We were rushed to the ambulance and driven at maddening speed through the shell-ridden town.

Though I was barely conscious, though I believed that I was nearing my last moments, I remember how it struck me vividly,—the contrast in the methods of fighting. German shells were blasting to pieces the shelter of wounded men and nurses. German wounded were being cared for by those whom their comrades sought to kill. The Hun might have killed his own. It did not matter. What is a life here or there to a Hohenzollern? And the Allies—here were two British stretcher-bearers bent under the burden of an enemy patient. They were striving to save his life from the fire of his own people.

I do not remember any more after I was put in the ambulance. I came to myself in a base hospital in France. I was strapped to a water bed. Everything round me was soft and fresh and clean, and smelled deliciously. There was a patient, sweet-smiling woman in nurse's costume who came and went to the beck and call of every man of us. We were whimpering and peevish; we were wracked with pain and weary of mind, but that nurse never failed to smile. Call a hundred times, call her once, she was always there to soothe, to help, to sympathize, and always smiling. Her heart must have been breaking at times, but her serene face never showed her sorrow or her weariness.

Often and often I am asked, "Why didn't you die when you were lying out there on the battle-field?" Why didn't I die? I could have, several times, but I didn't want to die, and I knew that if I were found I need not die.

We raw soldiers when we go to France are interested in the possibilities of being wounded. We know we've more or less got it coming to us, and we begin quietly to make inquiries. We notice all those men who wear the gold honor-bars on their sleeves. Yes; for every wound we get we have the right to wear a narrow strip of gold braid on the tunic sleeve.

We talk to the man with the honor-bar. We ask him how he was treated in the hospital. He may be doing the dirtiest fatigue duty round trench or camp, he may be smoking or writing a letter, but the minute be hears the word "hospital" he drops everything. If he be a Cockney soldier he will repeat the word: "'Orspital, mate—lor' luv ye, wish I wuz back!"

That is the feeling. Talk to a thousand men after this war; ask them their experiences and they will tell you a thousand different stories. Ask them how they were treated in the hospital and there is but one reply: "Treated in hospital? Excellent!"

There is only one word. The great Red Cross—Royal Army Medical Corps—is practically one hundred per cent. efficient. The veterans will tell the youngsters, "If you're wounded and have to lie out—then, lie out—

don't be foolish enough to die while you are lying out—because you can't die once they find you."

YOU CAN'T DIE.

We remember that. We remember facts, too, that we hear from time to time. We remember that out of all the casualties on the western front, only two and a half per cent. have died of wounds. We remember that we have a ninety-seven and a half fighting chance out of a hundred, and we are willing to take it. Some of us have read of other wars and we know, for instance, that in the American Civil War, from the best available statistics, over twenty-two per cent. died of wounds—and the reason? No efficient medical corps—no Red Cross—no neutral flag of red on white.

I was taken over to London as soon as I could be moved. I was in the Royal Herbert Hospital at Woolwich. It is not possible to describe in detail the treatment. The doctors were untiring. Hour after hour and day after day they worked without ceasing. The nurses were unremitting. No eight-hour day for them!

And here again I saw the treatment of the German wounded. They were in wards as gay with flowers, as cool, as clean, as delightful as ours. They had German newspapers to read, and certain days of the week brought a German band, drawn from among fit prisoners, to play German airs for the benefit of the sick prisoners. We think of this, and then we meet a British or French soldier who has been exchanged or who has escaped from a German hospital prison! It is hard to think of it calmly. The first impulse is to follow the law, "an eye for an eye and a tooth for a tooth." But that is not the way to-day of the square fighter.

At this hospital I was operated on and it was shown that it was an explosive bullet that hit me. Several pieces were taken out of me, and these I keep as grim souvenirs. Several other pieces are still in my body, and not infrequently by certain twinges I am made aware of their presence.

I have never seen an explosive bullet, and few of the Allied soldiers believe that many of us have felt them. Should one of the Allies be found making an explosive or Dum-Dum bullet, he is liable to be court-martialed and shot. There are those of us who would like to use them, but it is not what we like, it is what we may or may not do. It is discipline, and discipline forbids a brutal warfare. Thank God that we are fighting this war on the square, that our leaders are *making* us fight it on the square. Thank God that no attempt has ever been made to brutalize the troops of the Allies.

Part of the four months I was incapacitated was spent at Dobson Volunteer Red Cross Hospital, and here I was again struck with the marvelous devotion of the women. Day after day many of the leading women would come in, duchesses and others of title, and seek for Canadian lads to whom they could show kindnesses. Luxurious cars waited to drive us out for the air; flowers, fruits and books reached us, and quantities of cigarettes.

When the boys of the U.S.A. reach British hospitals in England, as no doubt they shall, they will find the same enthusiasm, the same attention bestowed upon them from the first ladies of the land and from the humblest who may only be able to give a smile, a cheery word or maybe a bunch of fragrant violets.

Two weeks before I was wounded I was recommended for a commission by my former colonel, Maynard Rogers, and the official document came to me while I was in the English hospital suffering from my wounds. It was a great source of pride and satisfaction that my commission, which I prize so highly to-day, was signed by the late Sir Charles Tupper, father of the Canadian Confederation and one of the Dominion's greatest statesmen.

But my fighting days are over. I am "out of it," but out with memories of good fellowship, real comrades, kindness, sympathy and friendships that dim the recollection of death, of destruction, of blood, of outrage, of murder and brutality.

CHAPTER XVI

GERMAN TERMINOLOGICAL
INEXACTITUDES

Some years ago a British statesman, then great, put on record a phrase which at once is polite and convincing. He wished to convey that a certain statement was a d—— lie, but as he himself had made the statement he was in somewhat of an awkward situation. He got out of the difficulty by calling it a "terminological inexactitude."

Now since I have been back in America, and more especially in the States, I have run to earth any number of terminological inexactitudes uttered by German propagandists. As far as Canada is concerned, the work is not now progressing very favorably. The German inexactitude farmer is sowing seed on barren soil. But I have traveled extensively during some crowded weeks through the States, and I find that among a certain section of the American public the seed of the German propagandist has taken root; not so deeply, however, but that an application of the hoe of truth will remove it. It is there all the same, and his success is spurring the agents to further efforts.

The German in high place is aware that the English are and always have been very friendly to the American people. He knows that the Englishman has regarded the American as of the same family. He also knows that one day, and possibly very soon, there will be a union that will amount almost to an amalgamation of the three greatest races on earth, closely bound now by ties of blood and friendship, that will never be broken: France, America, England. He knows that when that occurs the German day is done, that the sun has set forever on a German Empire.

The German in high place has realized this, and with the usual thoroughness of the race has set out to combat this friendship and prevent this joining. He is trying to do it by the regulation German method. He knows the British dislike of boasting, and that the American and the Britisher are woefully trusting. They themselves abhor deception and they distrust no man until they find him out. The British and the French have discovered the machinations of the German. The people of the United States have yet to be convinced that they have been deliberately deceived, cozened and duped by the Kaiser's government.

I am embarrassed at times as I go from town to town by the intensity of the congratulations poured on me as a representative of our Canadian Army.

"You Canadians have done it all. We know that. We know that the English are hanging back and have done nothing."

I am ashamed when people talk to me in such a strain. I am ashamed of their lack of intelligence, ashamed that they will allow themselves to be so deceived.

"You Canadians were asked by England to go and help her. When you got there they put you in front and stayed in safety themselves."

Think of it! Think of the base lie. Think of believing such twaddle. At first I did not trouble to deny the statement; then, as it was repeated again and again, I began to deny it.

The British Empire is in this fight. Canada is doing her share of it, and nothing more than her share. We were not asked to send men over. We declared war upon Germany ourselves, because we are an independent dominion. We have had on the battle-field at one time some one hundred and ten thousand men—that is the greatest number at any one time, though of course nearly five hundred thousand are in khaki. At Vimy Ridge we held the longest portion of trenches that we have ever held before or since—five miles. To right and left of us there were Imperial troops, Anzacs, Africans, and they held over fifty-five miles of line. We advanced four miles, and papers on this continent blazed with the news. The English advanced nine miles on the same day, and there was not so much as a paragraph about it on this side of the Atlantic.

For every overseas soldier wounded on the western front there are six of the Imperial troops wounded. This is true except at Lens, where the overseas casualties were considerably heavier.

All this about Canada being in front is a German "terminological inexactitude" which is so despicable that we in Canada are ashamed that it should be said of us. It will injure us after the war; it will injure our prestige in the empire, which is now higher than ever before. We are not boasters and egotists, we are fighters. We are fighting men who live straight and who are proud to fight straight, and who are disgusted at lies such as this.

The British, the Imperial troops, have done magnificently. They have done more than their share.

The original agreement with France was to place fifty thousand men in that country should Germany ever attack. The British have five million troops under arms, of which only one-fifth are overseas. They have some five hundred thousand more men in France than have the French themselves.

The British are fighting on many fronts. They are not fighting one war; they are fighting in German West Africa, they are in German East Africa. It was English troops who fought in the Cameroons. They are fighting in Mesopotamia and in Egypt. They have an army at Saloniki and in the Holy Land, and they have, of necessity, a large army in India, because the borders of that empire must be protected.

And then we hear that the English are not doing anything! The English are feeding their own prisoners in Germany, because the Germans were starving them. They have been keeping some of their Allies in munitions and money. They have been sheltering refugees from every nation that has been devastated and overrun by the mad Huns. They have Belgians and French and Serbians and Poles—a vast concourse of all nations is sheltered on the little island which is the Motherland. It would be a poor thing if the dominions could not protect themselves.

The British fleet has for three years kept the seas open for the neutral nations. The English fleet has protected Canada and other parts of the empire that have no navies of their own. The English must keep an army in England to protect her own shores. There was danger of invasion—that danger is past to all seeming, but it would not have passed had not the English had men on English soil.

"And, you know, we think it dreadful that our boys are being sent over to France to fight for democracy when England is keeping her men back in safety in England."

Another story this—another "terminological inexactitude." A fairly clever one. There is a half truth here. Yes; England has big reserves in England, and it's well for the world that she has. Well for the neutral world during these three years that England has her men in England.

The English have good reserves and they are in England. They are there because England is nearer to the firing line than is the base in France. They are there because it is easier to transport troops by boat across the English Channel, which is a matter of twenty-one miles, and another twenty or thirty miles in a train on the

French side, than it is to transport them in cattle cars over a congested railroad system from a base some twenty-six hours from the front line.

Can not the people who hear these stories disprove them for themselves? Is there not a war-map sold in America? England is closer to the firing line than are portions of France, the portions of France which are used as bases. It takes twenty minutes for a German air-ship to reach England.

Were the English soldiers all to be kept in France, in addition to being farther away from the line, they would still have to be fed. Is it better sense to keep them near to the food supply, or to send the reserves to France and use valuable tonnage to ship foodstuffs to them? There is no surplus food in France.

It makes me tired and it makes every Britisher the same to think that such absurd stories should take effect. Of course the German is keen enough to recognize that there is already the will to think evil of England. He just wishes to season it a little and stir it up. He is wily, is the German propagandist.

Then there is the hoary tale that England is keeping one hundred fifty thousand troops in Ireland to tyrannize over the poor Irish, while the States soldiers are sent to France to fight for democracy.

This I also thought too obvious a lie for denial, but it has been repeated and repeated again. I do not know whether there are any English regiments stationed in Ireland at all. There are good barracks in that country, and good camps, so there may be.

The Royal Irish Constabulary are quite able to cope at this time with any Sinn Fein disturbance which may arise. As far as the true Nationalist or Home Ruler is concerned, he has enlisted in British regiments and is fighting at the front. As far as the Ulsterman is concerned, he has enlisted long ago and is dead already or fighting still. The men of both sides who are over age are enlisted as Home Defense Volunteers, just as are the men of England, Scotland and Wales.

So little is there tyranny over Ireland that when the Conscription Bill was passed in the British Imperial Parliament it was enacted only for England, Scotland and Wales. If it had included Ireland some one might have made the accusation of tyranny.

In the United Kingdom there are no less freedom of action, freedom of speech and freedom of the individual than there are in America, and I include Canada in that word. They are as free as we, but they make no talk about it.

The United Kingdom, with the rest of the empire, is fighting to retain her own democracy. If Germany had won during the three years the Allies have held the safety of the world, then the world would have been under the heel of autocracy.

When I enlisted, and before I went over to England, I had no use for the Englishman myself; that was, the Englishman as we knew him in Western Canada. We had had specimens of "Algy boys," of "de Veres" and "Montmorency lads." These, we soon found out, were not the English true to type. They were ne'er-do-wells, remittance men, sent out of the way to the farthest point of the map.

In England we were treated with wonderful hospitality. I began to change my opinion, but not wholly until I reached France. There I met Tommy Atkins—the soldier and the gentleman. There is no cleaner, cooler, better sport on the fighting line than Mr. Atkins. Occasionally when the Irish are in a brilliant charge, when the Scotch punish the enemy with a bit of dogged fighting, it is reported. When the Canadians do a forward sprint the world rings with it. When the English advance and advance again and hold position and hold yet more positions, there is not a whisper of it—not a word.

I have no English blood in my veins, but I believe in fairness, I believe firmly that all the other nations of the empire put together have not done so much as have the English Tommies by themselves.

There has come about a complete change in the Canadian mind in its attitude to the English. If, before this war, there was ever a possibility of our breaking away from the empire, that possibility is now dead—dead and buried beyond recall.

This statement is not made at random. It is a considered sentence. At the Convention of the Great War Veterans' Association of Canada, the organization of the men returned from the world war, I was a delegate from my home town of Edmonton, Alberta. The first resolution at our first session was in effect—To propagate the good feeling between the dominions of the empire and between them and the Motherland; to continue the loyalty and devotion which have prompted us to fight for the old Union Jack.

After all, the voice of the men who have fought and bled for their country is the voice of the people.

Every criticism leveled at England or any other Ally from this side of the Atlantic is to throw a German stink-bomb for the Kaiser.

Feuds remembered are thoughts which are futile. The England of to-day is not the England of 1812. It is not possible to blame the man of to-day for the work of his great-grandfather. Read history and find out the nationality of the George who ruled in England in those far distant days. He was a German, spoke German, and could not read a word of the language of the country on whose throne he sat.

The Lloyd George of ten years ago was the most hated and hooted man in Britain. He is not the Lloyd George of ten years ago to-day, he is the Lloyd George of the present—the most loved and respected man on earth.

The American people and the British are fundamentally alike. They are of the one stock. They have the same ideals and principles. If the English did not make sacrifices in other days, to-day they are making a sacrifice as great, or maybe greater, than others of the Allies.

The joining of the peoples of America and Britain in a tie which can never be broken is imminent. The knot is in the making.

In keeping with the dastardly methods of "frightfulness" in Europe, the German propagandist has thought on this side to strike at the women—to terrify the mothers.

It is terribly hard for women to let their men go. We know that. Our women know it, but they are ashamed should one of their men attempt to hold back. The German lie-mongers whisper: "It is the last time you will see your boy. It is certain death on the western front."

It is not so. The Canadian troops altogether have used up some four hundred fifty thousand in three years. Of this number, in the three years of severe fighting, only five per cent. have been killed. Of the four and a half million, approximately, who have been wounded in the fighting of three years, only two and a half per cent. have died of their wounds.

It is bad enough, but it is not nearly so bad as the German scare manufacturer would seek to make out. Boys come through without a scratch. Not many, certainly, but they come through. There is every reason to believe that you will get your boy back. There is still more reason to believe that if you hold that thought before him while he is still with you, and hold that thought before yourself when he is gone, he will come back.

Women have a tremendous responsibility in this war. Wars are always women's wars, mothers' wars. We boys have courage and we need it, but we also need the greater courage of those women we have left behind to back us up. They have to bear the brunt of the war, which to them is a fight of endurance and eternal, everlasting waiting—waiting—waiting.

Do not think of the sorrow of his leaving, think of the pride of his going.

The martial spirit is not actively abroad on this side of the Atlantic yet. Wait till the boys get over to France; wait till they see the outrages on women and on nature, and all the blood of their fighting ancestors will boil with indignation and rage. They will thank God that they have come to prevent such a devastation on the soil of their own homeland.

In the trenches the boys compare the merits of their mothers. It is a wonderful thing, that spirit of mother love which surrounds us, blesses us and leads us on to higher things. We gather together in the trench and we talk of mother—mother—mother. The lad whose mother cried and fainted when he left quietly drops out from the group. We always know him. He is just a tiny bit afraid that we will ask him how his mother sent him off. He never shows his letters from home, because it is possible that she writes him laments and moanings. He is ashamed. But those of us who have a home courage of which we talk—how we boast! Mother is a mighty factor in the winning of the war.

Out to France we go for Flag and Country. "Over the top" we go for Mother. And mother, that one simple word, embraces the whole of womanhood.

Remember that your boy is going for you. Talk to the French mother, to the English mother, who has lost all. Ask her about the war, about peace. "Peace, yes, we all want peace, but not a German peace. If all the menfolk die and there is no one else to go, why, we will carry on!"

And here I want to ask: What is the pacifist in this country doing for peace? Nothing. He is only trying to put off this war, for a worse war. Every man, woman or child who talks peace before the complete defeat of Germany is a Kaiser agent, spreading German poison gas to the injury and possible destruction of his own countrymen.

Back at home we must have the United Spirit which is inspiring us at the front. After all, it is not the body which is going to take us through to ultimate victory; it is the Spirit. And because American arms ultimately will be the deciding factor in this war, so will American womanhood. From what I have seen already, I have no hesitation in saying that the American mother will be just as true to herself as the English and French mother has been.

Let him go with a smile, and if you can't smile, whistle. You can never know how much it means to him. We at the front are undaunted. If there ever had been a thought of defeat, to-day, with the American arms beside us, we are certain of a sure and glorious victory.

Because we know that if Cæsar crossed the Rhine for Rome, and Napoleon crossed it for France and autocracy, so shall we, the Freemen of the world, not only cross the Rhine, but will march even to Berlin for the sake of Liberty, of Love, of Right and of Democracy.

CHAPTER XVII

THE LAST CHAPTER

by

"HERSELF"

War! It was the first of August, 1914, and I almost ran home from the city to tell the news to my people.

War! It was like we'd be in it. War between England and Germany. That war we had all heard of and knew was inevitable. The war of the ages was imminent.

I had been free-lancing in Fleet Street for the past three months. Left *The Daily Chronicle* over the Home Rule questions, as well as other things.

I was in Ireland for the Ulster gun-running. Ireland was a seething mass of German-inspired sedition south of the Boyne. The authorities apparently would not listen to the warnings of Ulster. But Ulster was ready for anything. There were hospitals, clearing stations, bases. There were despatch riders, signalers, transport men, all in readiness, besides the ordinary infantry volunteers, who were pledged by all means in their power to keep Ireland under the flag of the Union.

I was in a little country church one Sunday morning. A roll of a drum and the skirl of a fife came wafting across the valley on the April breeze. The minister paused a moment in his sermon. Two, three, half a dozen men rose and softly left. They were going to the rendezvous in case of alarm. No one knew what might happen. A conflagration might flare out at a moment's notice.

But in August there came war, real war. Civilization was threatened. Ulster handed over men, guns, ammunition, hospitals and nurses to the Imperial government. Hundreds of the Ulster Volunteers in the Ulster Division have died for Britain. Hundreds of the men south of the Boyne who have not been bitten with the microbe of revolution, and a mistaken idea that England is a tyrant, have died for the cause of world Liberty.

How we lived through those first electric four days of August! Would the Liberal government funk? We doubted them unjustly. Then came the devastation of Belgium, and Britain gave Germany its disappointment—Britain declared war. Ireland rallied round the brave old Union Jack; the colonies, rather we call them now the dominions overseas, India, Africa, Canada, Australia, New Zealand and the smaller islands, sent word that they were with us to a man.

And then the fight commenced. Those casualty lists of the first Imperial Army! God in Heaven! The thud of distant guns, and then nearer and nearer we could hear in London the rumble of the enemy artillery as though of thunder. Smoke drifted over, and we lived in a pall of death.

It was in October that Fate's apparent working showed itself.

"This war will alter our lives very greatly," said my aunt one evening in this month, as we sat around the fire. We have all a trace of second sight. Most old families of the north of Ireland can claim to be "fey."

"It will," said I, "for free-lancing is getting played out. I shall have to get steady work."

No more was said, and no special work came my way. It was useless to attempt to train for nursing. I had no aptitude for that, and munition workers of our sex were not called yet.

Then the Canadians came. The First Contingent. For the most part big, strong, hefty-looking men; well uniformed, well set up. Eighty-seven per cent. of them Old Country born.

Among them my cousin, Peter Watson. Dear old man Peter, I wonder do you know of my happiness which is the outcome of your journey "West"? I wish you might know it, and share some of the joy. Yours was a lonely and a sensitive soul.

Peter had been in the Suffolks. A lieutenant in the Imperial Army. Money was scarce and he threw up his commission. He tried Canada as a fortune making ground. Lingered a while in Calgary, and when war broke out enlisted in the now famous Fighting Tenth.

Peter came up from Salisbury to see us. He met me in town a few times. We lunched, dined, did a theater. He brought pals with him. There was Sandy Clark. Poor old Sandy! I have his collar badge C10. Another soldier took it off his tunic for me before they buried him. A sniper got Sandy in June, 1916.

There was Farmer. He was a signaler, and was transferred. I saw his name listed killed, too. I don't know where. There were half a dozen other Canadian boys, Peter and myself. We lunched one day at Pinoli's in Rupert Street. We pledged to our next meeting after the war at the same place. We shan't meet at Pinoli's. There is none of the boys alive. I only live of all the party. It was a strange thing that day. I did not know it would be the last time I should see Peter, but he came back from down the street and kissed me "good-by" a second time. I wondered. Old man Peter.

The war has come home to our family. There is none of us left. Tom Small, my step-brother, is still living and still fighting. I pray his safety to the end. They all went, one after the other. The last to go was Hugh. July, 1916, on the eleventh day he was killed. Dear old boy, it is unrealizeable yet. You won the military Cross and you won yet another undying honor. You were sniped in the glory of completing a fine piece of work. Your six feet of glorious young manhood lie deep in French soil. Good-by, Hugh!

Peter was reported missing. All of us who were left alive tried every means of which we knew and of which we heard to find a trace of him. We got none. At last I decided that an advertisement in a daily paper would bring replies from wounded soldiers. I advertised in *The Daily Express*. The advertisement appeared on a Wednesday, and on the Thursday morning I had a letter from a young Canadian soldier of the Third Battalion who was in the Royal Herbert Hospital at Woolwich. He told me of knowing something of what may have happened to Peter. The possibilities were that he was blown up in company with a trench full of other soldiers.

There is little reason to doubt this awful ending to a young life; there is no evidence of anything else.

The letter of the young Canadian soldier was kindly and frank in tone. I answered it, and asked if he had any relations in the Old Country. He replied that he had not, and we decided that we would go and see him in hospital and try in some way to help him in his loneliness.

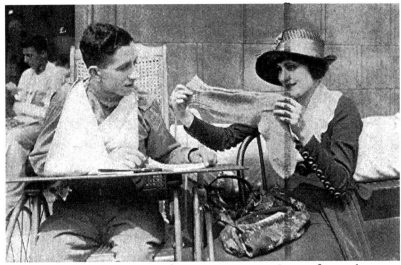

©Famous Players—Lasky Corporation. Scene from the Photo-Play "THEY LOOK BIG ENOUGH, DON'T THEY?"

A close shave in Flanders

Before seeing the soldier I received several other letters, notably from Sam J. Peters, who came to see us, and was positive that he knew Peter as a man who had aided him on his being wounded himself. Lance-Corporal Carey was another who wrote, and Corporal George A. Vowel, known as Black Jack, then of the Tenth and now of the Thirteenth Machine Gun Corps, wrote a kindly letter.

On a Saturday afternoon we went down to Woolwich, and after a short chat with a nurse in charge were allowed to see the Canadian who had written first. Private Harold R. Peat was slight, small, and looked almost emaciated. We talked for some time and he showed us several souvenirs which he had. We liked him, and promised to come back. He agreed that he would get a pass for the following Sunday so that we could see him in the regulation hours.

He mentioned during conversation how he had seen the advertisement in *The Daily Express,* and how he always had the desire to comfort those who had lost relatives, especially when all the official information could give was "missing."

On the next day it occurred to me that the days must hang long on such a boy's hands, and I forthwith wrote him a card with some small joke on it. He replied by a letter. Soon we wrote to each other every day. It was quite amusing, and at times our letters amounted to a war of wits and repartee.

Our friendship grew, and then he got well enough to leave the hospital. We wrote regularly, but finally there were more hospital visits to make when, as a paralyzed wreck of a youth, he was sent back from France. Private Peat rallied quickly, and to my astonishment one day he walked in to see me at the offices where the Efficiency Engineers had their headquarters.

"Time for me to come and see you!" he exclaimed. I brought him into the reception room, left him for two minutes until I made some arrangements as to work.

When I returned he was in a faint, from which it took some time to rouse him. His convalescent camp was in the country, and he had trudged some five miles of muddy road in the rain in his endeavor to reach a railway station with the ultimate object in view of visiting me.

We saw each other frequently from this time. My dear friend, Amy Naylor, jokingly warned me: "Be careful, Bebe, you are playing with fire." I laughed. I had other ideas, but nevertheless her words made me think. I found out that I, for one, was not playing. It remained to find out whether the other party to the game believed it a pastime, or something of more moment.

Soon there came word that certain of the disabled men were to be returned to Canada for discharge. Private Peat was among them. He had word that he would soon receive a commission, though he would not again be fit for active service.

Without one word spoken, it came to be understood between us that it would only be a matter of time before I would go to Canada to join him. Fate seemed to arrange the matter silently that at some indefinite time when "he" had had time to look around and "see how things were," he would send for me.

It was a matter of weeks before I got a cable: "Come now." I came.

We met through tragedy. My husband has all the sacredness to me of having come back to me from the brink of the grave. He has all the wonder of a man who has offered, and is willing to offer his life again for right. He has all the glory of a man who had not to be "fetched." He went.

He is friend, pal and husband all in one. Of Peter, the unconscious instrument of Fate's working, we must say of him but one thing: "He died for his country."

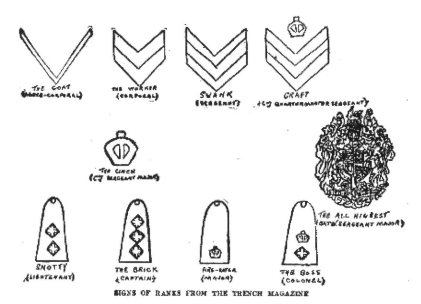

SIGNS OF RANKS FROM THE TRENCH MAGAZINE

SIGNS OF RANKS FROM THE TRENCH
MAGAZINE

THE TEN COMMANDMENTS OF A SOLDIER WHILE ON ACTIVE SERVICE

1. When on guard thou wilt challenge all parties approaching thee.

2. Thou shalt not send any engraving nor any likeness of any air-ship in Heaven above or on any postcard of the Earth beneath, nor any drawing of any submarine under the sea, for I, the Censor, am a jealous Censor, visiting the iniquities of the offenders with three months C.B., but showing mercy unto thousands by letting their letters go free who keep my commandments.

3. Thou shalt not use profane language unless under extraordinary circumstances, such as seeing your comrade shot, or getting coal oil in your tea.

4. Remember the soldier's week consists of seven days: six days shalt thou labor and do all thy work, and on the seventh do all thy odd jobs.

5. Honor your President and your Country, keep your rifle oiled and shoot straight that thy days may be long upon the land which the enemy giveth thee.

6. Thou shalt not steal thy comrade's kit.

7. Thou shalt not kill—TIME.

8. Thou shalt not adulterate thy mess tin by using it as a shaving mug.

9. Thou shalt not bear false witness against thy comrades but preserve a strict neutrality on his outgoings and his incomings.

10. Thou shalt not covet thy sergeant's post, nor the corporal's nor the staff major's, but do thy duty and by dint of perseverance rise to the high position of major general.

SOME THINGS THAT WE OUGHT AND OUGHT NOT TO SEND

Candies, cigarettes—and ordinary, plain cigarettes are good enough, so long as you send plenty. If he chews, send him chewing. Cigarettes are an absolute necessity because they are the only things soothing to the nerves when under heavy shell fire. Powdered milk in small quantities, or Horlick's Milk Tablets, are always welcome. Pure jam; don't ever make a mistake in this and send plum and apple, because if he ever gets back alive, he will surely take your life for making such a terrible mistake—different fruit preserves they long for. Never send corned beef. This would be even a worse crime than the plum and apple jam. A pair of sox, home-made and pure wool, you ought to send once a week, because you must remember the Red Cross takes care only of the wounded men and not the fighters in the trenches; the government and home folks must look after the fighter in the field. Three-finger mittens knitted up to the elbow, with the first finger absolutely bare, are very welcome. Scarfs are quite unnecessary. Tommy usually gives these to the French lassies. Different insect powders Tommy likes to get, because he can't buy these out there. There is no doubt about it that, although we get used to the "cooties," yet sometimes they outnumber us and it is necessary to put a gas attack over on them.

Strong powders are the only thing. Candles, matches, and if possible small alcoholic burners are very essential things. Of course, if you send him a burner it would be necessary for you to keep sending him alcohol, because this can't be bought in France. Nor can we get sugar out there. Any of these things with a nice long "letter" will delight Tommy or Sammy or Poilou.

Image 1. *Canadian troops leaving for France* (1919) [Photograph] At: http://www.gwpda.org/photos/coppermine/displayimage .php?album=13&pos=147

14204003R00159

Printed in Great Britain
by Amazon